Your CRYSTAL PLAN

75 CRYSTALS TO UNBLOCK YOUR PATH AND ACHIEVE YOUR PURPOSE

Gemma Petherbridge

GODSFIELD

First published in Great Britain in 2024
by Godsfield Press, an imprint of Octopus
Publishing Group Ltd, Carmelite House,
50 Victoria Embankment, London EC4Y 0DZ
www.octopusbooks.co.uk

An Hachette UK Company
www.hachette.co.uk

Distributed in the US by Hachette Book
Group, 1290 Avenue of the Americas,
4th and 5th Floors, New York, NY 10104

Distributed in Canada by Canadian Manda
Group, 664 Annette St, Toronto, Ontario,
Canada M6S 2C8

ISBN 978-1-84181-560-2

A CIP catalogue record for this book is
available from the British Library.

Printed and bound in China.

10 9 8 7 6 5 4 3 2 1

Staff credits
Commissioning Editor: Nicola Crane
Art Director: Yasia Williams
Designer: Claire Huntley
Senior Editor: Leanne Bryan
Copyeditor: Caroline Taggart
Picture Researchers: Giulia Hetherington
    & Jen Veall
Assistant Production Manager: Lisa Pinnell

MIX
Paper | Supporting
responsible forestry
FSC® C008047
www.fsc.org

Picture credits
For Conscience Crystals: Photography by
Gemma Petherbridge 163; Holly Booth 1, 6,
11, 16, 19, 23, 26, 35, 41, 91, 137, 175, 195, 205;
Sarah Ann Wright 24, 63, 71, 87, 93, 123, 125,
129, 135, 141, 145, 149, 151, 157, 197.

For Octopus Publishing Group: 9, Giulia
Hetherington 59; Michael Illas 61, 65, 73–85,
95–103, 107, 109, 113, 117, 127, 131, 133, 139, 153,
155, 159, 161, 165–73, 177, 179–87, 193, 201, 203.

Alamy Stock Photo: Eduardo Estellez 105,
Pillyphotos 69, Science Photo Library 67,
Valery Voennyy 207; Dreamstime.com:
Björn Wylezich 121, Mohamed El-Jaouhari
89, Montree Nanta 199, Vvoevale 115, 119,
189; Getty Images: Kinga Krzeminska 20;
iStock Photo: Picteorico 13, SageElyse 147;
Shutterstock Creative: Finesell 143, Gozzoli
111, Roy Palmer 97, 191.

Disclaimer
No medical claims are made for crystals
in this book and information given is not
intended to act as a substitute for medical
treatment. Healing means bringing mind,
body and spirit back into balance, it does
not imply a cure.

Sourcing crystals responsibly
Remember that crystals are a gift from
Mother Earth, so please respect her and
source your crystals responsibly. Ethical
sourcing means educating yourself about
where your crystals have come from, how
they have been mined and the supply chain
they have come through. The more we
ask these questions, the more the crystal
industry will realize how important these
factors are to their customers.

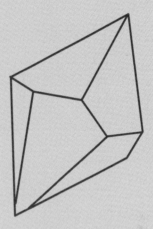

To my sister and the women in my life
who have always campaigned my corner.

And to the crystal community, both known
and unknown. May this book deepen your passion
for crystals even more.

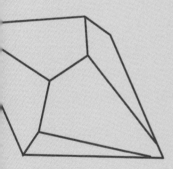

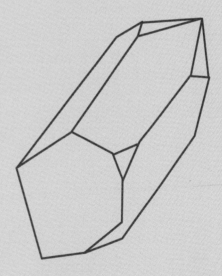

Contents

How to Use This Book

Welcome – this book was written for you and all our fellow crystal fans, to alleviate the number-one worry the crystal community has, which is choosing the wrong crystal.

Originally presented as a workshop, the crystal plan process detailed in this book will only take you an afternoon to learn. Once you know it, you can implement the steps quickly by returning to the book time and again to choose your perfect crystal.

In the first section (see pages 8–27) I lay the foundations by exploring why you would work with crystals and how they support us, using the most popular and widely used techniques. I also offer some background information on the chakras and what a 'purpose' is. Both will be useful to you later in the book.

In the second section (see pages 28–45) we start creating your crystal plan. You will be guided to identify your goals, before learning how to read the chakras to help pinpoint the colour of the crystal you need. Then, in the third section (see pages 46–55), you will use the intuitive skills that I'll be teaching you to choose your crystal.

Once you have identified your ideal crystal, in the fourth section (see pages 56–207) you will find a double-page spread telling you all about it and the techniques to use with it.

The crystal plan process breaks down goals into *physical, emotional* and *soul-aligned*. If you are reading this book for the first time I recommend starting with a physical goal (one that supports the physical body). As this is the quickest to do, it will give you the chance to see how the whole process works.

My hope is that the crystal plan process will empower you to deepen your connection to crystals so that you can see them as the magical tools we know they are.

So find yourself a notebook and pen and let's begin...

Your Crystal Plan

Crystals are energy tools we can use to support emotional and physical healing, but also to help us achieve our goals and dreams. The problem is it can be hard to understand which crystal to use and how to work with it. This becomes even more complex when we realize the crystal we need depends on our own unique energies and current life situation.

Your Crystal Plan solves all of these concerns by guiding you through a simple process to help you find that ideal crystal. From there you can learn the best ways to work with it to get the kind of support you need.

WHAT KIND OF GOALS CAN I CREATE A CRYSTAL PLAN FOR?

Your goal can be about anything you want. But no matter what it is, it will always fit into one of our three categories:

Physical purpose goals: These are goals that support the physical body. You can use crystals to support and heal the body as well as to strengthen it, increase your energy levels and work towards optimum health.

Emotional purpose goals: These are connected to both your emotional body and your mental health. You might focus on this type of goal when you are looking to overcome a fear or phobia, to heal a limiting belief or to feel more confident.

Soul purpose goals: This type of goal is closely linked to your hopes and dreams and will include your spiritual development and what you want to manifest and bring into your life.

WHY IS THE CRYSTAL PLAN PROCESS SO POWERFUL?

The process draws on the skills of both sides of the brain to help us choose our crystals. From the goal-setting stage up to the moment we identify the colour of the crystal we need, we use the left brain to evaluate our options. Then, when using our intuition to choose the crystal, we are drawing on the right side of our brain. This is connected to our subconscious where a lot of our hidden programming resides. Accessing this information helps to deepen the healing because we can work on the core issue.

We are attracted to crystals with the frequency that will best support us (see page 10 for more about this). Therefore when we enter a crystal shop and a particular crystal stands out to us, that is our intuition's way of highlighting what we need. Intuition is a right-brain activity, so using it to choose our crystals means we are working on those subconscious issues.

Why Work with Crystals?

We are attracted to crystals for two reasons: their beauty and their stable energy. If you put a crystal under a powerful microscope, you will see that its atoms are made up of one or more minerals repeating in exactly the same way. This consistency gives crystals a very stable frequency, and also means they have a low state of *entropy*: they don't change when they are subject to stress.

In contrast, the human body requires different atomic structures for different areas. This means we are made up of multiple different frequencies, so our state of entropy is much higher even on a normal day. When stressors enter our life we become more reactive.

In order to be happy, healthy and have positive emotions we want a high frequency. When our frequency is reduced, our emotions become more and more negative. Plus, a lower frequency in the body can result in illness. Science shows that a lower frequency will resonate and start to match a higher frequency, so bringing a crystal with a higher frequency into our environment can stabilize and even heighten our own frequency. Using our knowledge of the chakras and their associated colours (see page 13), we can choose crystals with a frequency that matches our goals.

These simple facts are the reason the crystal plan process is so effective. With this knowledge we can deliberately choose crystals to support our physical, emotional and soul-aligned goals.

CLEANSING CRYSTALS

When you cleanse a crystal you are releasing from it any energy it might have taken on. This is a popular practice that a majority of crystal collectors carry out, especially as it helps you build a connection with your crystals. Personally, I don't put extra pressure on myself to regularly cleanse my crystals because their state of entropy is so low that they will rarely take anything on.

I would, however, always cleanse a crystal that I'm asking to take on negative energy for me. For example on page 134 I talk about Malachite taking on emotional or physical pain, so after a treatment, that energy needs to be removed from the crystal.

Not all cleansing techniques can be used on all crystals, so below I'm showing you three that can. They only take a few minutes; while you are doing them, make sure you have the intention in mind that you are removing unwanted energy from that crystal.

Saging: Light a sage stick. After a moment, blow it out and allow the smoke to pass around all areas of the crystal.

Sound: You can use one frequency (sound) to clear another frequency (the crystal's vibration). Simply sound chimes or other music over the crystal.

White light: Cup your crystal between both hands and imagine white light coming from your hand, surrounding the crystal.

An Introduction to the Chakras

Everything is made of energy. That means human beings are energy as well. Ancient communities have known this truth for thousands of years. The Vedas, ancient Indian texts, present the idea that we have multiple bodies: the causal body, which houses our higher self (the soul part of us that has lived many lives); the subtle body, comprising the intuitive, emotional and energetic parts of us; and the gross or physical body.

The suggestion of a subtle, energetic body isn't limited to the teachings of the Vedas. Indigenous Americans, Ancient Egyptians, the Inca and Mayan civilizations as well as Buddhism and far eastern mysticism all offer similar concepts. Each has its own terminology for the energy that flows through the body – *prana, qi/ki/chi, mana* or life force energy – but these terms all mean substantially the same thing.

Like the physical body, which is made up of multiple systems (such as the skeletal, nervous and respiratory systems), the energy body consists of many parts that together create our aura. This is an energetic field, also known as the auric field, that surrounds all living things.

WHAT ARE THE CHAKRAS?

At the heart of the energy body is the chakra system. Chakra is the Sanskrit word for 'wheel' and the chakras are energetic discs that constantly filter the energies and emotions we experience, before storing or releasing them.

Many people believe there are numerous chakras, but we will focus on the seven main ones, which run up the spine through the head to the crown. Each one represents an area of the body, as well as specific life stages and the lessons we begin to explore at those times.

A fully open, healthy chakra is described as *balanced*. Over time different events and experiences might deplete one disc, causing it to be *blocked*.

Alternatively, too much energy in a disc makes it *overactive*. Blocked or overactive chakras can then affect the flow of energy through the body, showing up as all kinds of emotional or physical ailments as well as a depleted ability to manifest and achieve our goals.

Each chakra vibrates at a different frequency and, as colours are also a vibration, each chakra has a correlating colour. To heal the energy body we can offer that chakra more of the colour it needs. That includes working with crystals of that colour. This book is going to show you how to do that.

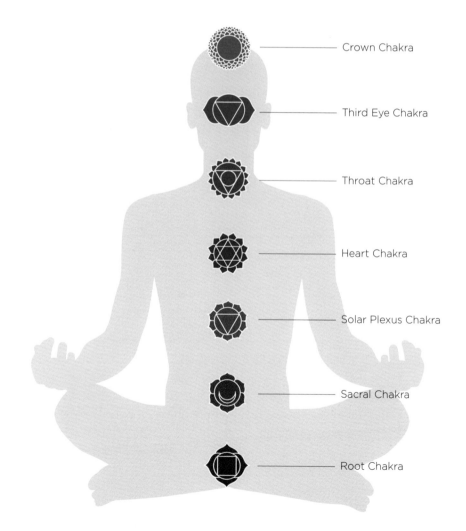

Crown Chakra

Third Eye Chakra

Throat Chakra

Heart Chakra

Solar Plexus Chakra

Sacral Chakra

Root Chakra

What Is a Purpose?

Many cultures believe we come to Earth with a plan, a 'soul blueprint' of experiences, interactions and achievements we want to work through. This plan is created in the time between lives, but when we reincarnate it is forgotten so we can authentically carry out the lessons without any awareness that they might be happening in the future.

The concept of *dharma* is also part of the Vedic teachings. This is a Sanskrit word that, when translated, speaks of our *soul purpose* – the reasons our soul chose to reincarnate into the world, including the lessons we want to learn and how we want to support humanity and the planet while we are here.

In other words, we are all here for a reason and we all have a purpose.

WHY IS A PURPOSE SO IMPORTANT?

In essence, our purpose is the answer to the biggest of life's questions: why are we here?

Most people want to be happier, and realizing your purpose is how you get there. You might have heard the expression *being in the flow*. When you have realized your soul purpose, it raises your vibration so that you live in a state of joy or bliss. From there, blocks are limited and what you want to achieve manifests in your life instantly. This is being in your 'flow'.

Imagine a ballerina performing on stage in front of an audience – it looks effortless. That is what being in the flow looks like, but it would have taken years of hard work for a dancer to get to that point. If you already know your purpose and are working towards it, you might recognize this. Yes, it involves work, learning lessons and overcoming obstacles (the lessons your soul wanted you to learn), but the outcome is living in effortless flow. We all deserve to live life in this state, but your success is more than just the realization of your own purpose.

You will become a shining light for your loved ones and others in your community who are also waking up to the idea of living their purpose. And life lived with purpose has a ripple effect. It's clear that the modern world is going through dramatic changes. Raising the vibration of Mother Earth is a way to make positive change, so when you individually embody your purpose, you are also increasing the vibration of the whole planet.

AWAKENING TO YOUR PURPOSE

If you are reading a crystal book like this one, it's likely you are firmly on a self-development and spiritual path. I imagine you can remember a time before your spiritual awakening when you might unknowingly have let life happen to you. When we are in this state, we are living unconsciously, making choices that society says are right for us but often finding that the outcome leaves us feeling empty, numb and unfulfilled. The majority of people in this situation will start to ask, 'Is there more to life?'

Those starting to make more conscious decisions are deemed *self-aware*: they realize that the unhealthy or unconscious choices they make often result in negative physical and emotional outcomes.

From self-awareness, we move into *self-improvement* and start making changes to our physical and emotional bodies so we can heal and strengthen them. This is always going to result in us feeling happier, more content and more in control of our lives. However, that only gets us so far. The feeling of wanting more from life will still be there. That realization triggers a *spiritual awakening* and a reconnection to our soul.

This is the moment when we search for meaning at a deeper, soul level and the exploration into our spiritual development begins. It starts with a drive to soak up as much information as possible. Then over time we pinpoint the aspects of spirituality we love the most and refine them into a soul purpose. This is a lifestyle that encapsulates all our passions, so we can live a fulfilled life aligned with our soul blueprint.

Crystal Techniques

Crystals are not just display pieces. Our ancestors knew what a powerful tool for change they could be. In the coming pages I'm going to show you numerous ways you can work with them. Please try them all, as this will deepen your knowledge of them and your awareness of the energies around you. Over time you will find your favourite techniques and will use them the most.

Whether you are making crystal elixirs, crystal grids or placing crystals on your body, my aim is to show you the classic techniques so you can understand the basic principles. From there you can build on them, adding your own flourishes of personality. For example, I've seen people paint images of their crystal grid formations so that they can display them permanently in their home. Some use crystal elixirs in their smoothies and some make their own crystal jewellery, keeping their favourite stones with them throughout the day.

In Working with Your Crystals (see pages 56–207) I have outlined three techniques per crystal, one each for physical, emotional and soul-aligned support. For these I have considered the crystal's properties and energy levels and the best way to work with that particular crystal for each of the goal types. But you can also choose a technique from this section.

CRYSTAL MEDITATION

Meditating with crystals is particularly powerful because the relaxation process shifts our nervous system from a stressed *sympathetic* state into the *parasympathetic* state known as *rest and digest*. From this place our bodies are more receptive to healing work. Sitting in silence with a new crystal is the perfect way to see how working with it will affect our energies.

The changes a crystal can offer are normally subtle, so a simple five-minute meditation that involves lengthening the breath allows us to understand how we will feel a crystal's energy.

We all receive energy differently, but the most common reactions are:

Physical: A tickling sensation, feeling hot or cold, becoming aware of an area of the body, a change in heart rate or a gurgling tummy.

Emotional: A shift in emotions, sense of peace, tears, memory recall or remembering a certain fear, limiting belief or anxiety that needs healing.

CRYSTAL HEALING MEDITATION

1. As you sit comfortably on your yoga mat or a chair, hold your crystal in your dominant hand (your right hand if you are right-handed, left if you are left-handed).

2. Close your eyes and start counting your breath. You want to lengthen both the inhale and the exhale; if your normal breath is a count of three, start increasing it to a count of four or five.

3. Once you feel more relaxed, imagine a ray of light, the same colour as the crystal, coming out from it and surrounding you.

4. Stay there for a few minutes enjoying the energy.

5. Then when you are ready, see the energy go back into the crystal and open your eyes.

CRYSTAL LAYOUTS

One of the best and easiest ways to work with crystals is to place them directly on to the parts of the body that need healing. Like the meditation practices on the previous page, you first focus on relaxing the body so it can receive the energies more deeply. Then lie down and place one or multiple crystals in specific areas to evoke energy changes.

Within the crystal property pages (see pages 56–207) I suggest many different crystal layouts. Here I'm going to guide you through the steps for the best-known of them, the chakra balance. Later in the book (see pages 46–55) you will have the chance to select your own chakra crystal set. This is a set of seven crystals, one for each of the main chakras. After you have chosen your set, refer to this guide so that you can do a full chakra balance once a month. This keeps the chakras healthy and free from any energetic build-up.

CRYSTAL CHAKRA BALANCE

Make sure your crystals are to hand and your room is warm, as you will be lying down for 20 minutes.

1. Lie down with a blanket over you and your head on a pillow. Starting at the root chakra, move up the body, placing crystals on each energy point. The crystals you use need to match that chakra's colour (for reference, see the chakra diagram on page 13).

2. Add the crown chakra crystal last. This goes on your pillow, about 2.5cm (1in) above your head.

3. Once you have added all crystals, stay in this position for 20 minutes. If crystals move or fall off, don't put them back on, as that is a sign that they have done their job.

4. Once the 20 minutes are up, remove the crystals, starting with the one at the crown chakra, then moving down the body.

5. Sit up slowly, giving yourself a moment to allow your energy body to relax before you stand up.

WEARING CRYSTALS

On the previous page I spoke about placing crystals on specific areas of the body to solicit healing. We can also choose to wear them or carry them in our pockets, wallets or bags to keep the healing going much longer. This is a cost-effective, simple and practical way to work with crystals, as it offers sustainable support. However, there are two rules you need to follow to ensure you are doing this correctly:

Rule one: Only carry crystals with you if they can be positioned close to or over the chakra they are supporting. This is an important consideration, as you want to be enhancing your energies, not stifling them with a contrasting frequency. For help with this go to page 13 to see what chakra your crystal's colour relates to and the area of the body it needs to be positioned over.

Rule two: Some crystals, such as tektites and Black Obsidian, have a busy frequency that could stress the nervous system if you keep them with you for long periods. In those cases, wearing your jewellery for a few hours will be enough.

DISPLAYING CRYSTALS

Where you place a crystal in the home can affect the energies of that space and how people feel and behave there. Considering the placement of a crystal in your home is particularly useful if you like investing in larger statement pieces. Taking the time to consider the kind of energies you would like in each room will help you make the most of your investment.

To maximize the impact of your new crystal on your surroundings and to allow it to support you the best way it can, you should ideally place it in a space that directly matches its properties. Therefore, motivational crystals offering strength, vitality and a wish to fulfil your goals are best in a work environment. In contrast, crystals that support self-care and compassion are perfect in a bathroom and those that calm and offer peace are ideal on a bedside table.

> Crystals with intense energy are best stored in cabinets, drawers or a crystal pounch. This disconnects you from their energy when you are not working with them.

WHERE TO BEST DISPLAY YOUR CRYSTALS IN THE HOME	
ROOM/SPACE	CRYSTAL COLOURS
Entrance hall	Black, pink, blue, white
Living room/reception room	Black, pink, green, blue, white
Kitchen	Red, orange, yellow
Bedroom	Green, pink, purple
Office/workspace	Red, orange, yellow, blue
Bathroom	Green, pink, purple
Study/meditation space	Purple, white, transparent

CRYSTAL TALISMANS

We can use crystals as a talisman (a physical object we can wear or display that reminds us of our current goal so we stay focused on it). A crystal talisman is the quintessential good-luck charm, because the energy it offers matches your goal, keeping it at the forefront of your mind. You could use your talisman in a ritual to mark the start of your project, welcoming in the right energies and connecting to your intention and your crystal so your project begins with some positive momentum behind it.

CRYSTAL TALISMAN RITUAL

1. Cleanse your crystal, freeing it of any old energies.

2. With a paper and pen, journal:
   - What you want the outcome of your goal to be.
   - How you will know you have achieved that goal.
   - How achieving this goal will make you feel.

3. Fold the paper in half.

4. Now, hold the crystal in your non-dominant hand, close your eyes and imagine the outcome and how you will feel.

5. After a few moments, open your eyes and place the folded paper where you want to display the crystal. Then put the crystal on top.

6. Light a candle next to it. This represents inviting guidance to show you the best way forwards.

7. Now it's time to start your project.

Some crystals are carved into the form of deities, gods, goddesses and spirit animals so they can represent the properties or archetype of that figure. A crystal carving like this would also be a good talisman.

CRYSTAL GRIDS

A crystal grid is the original vision board: a collage of images depicting the things we want to attract and bring into our life. We display the collage so that we can take a moment each day to imagine what it would feel like to have those things already. Visualizing like this aligns our energies so that those aspirations can enter our life easily.

The shapes of the grid are designed to attract and funnel our aspirations towards us. For this we use *sacred geometry*: shapes found throughout nature that depict the mathematics of the Universe. These shapes are found in the atomic structure of the crystals and are replicated in the shape of the grid. When we work with objects that have sacred geometry within them, we are aligning our goals with the energies of the Universe.

There are numerous shapes and grid layouts you can try. In Working with Your Crystals (see pages 56–207) I will suggest more formations, but here I am going to show you how to create a classic hexagonal grid. Some grid shapes have specific energetic themes, but a hexagon can be used for any theme.

PREPARATION

Start by deciding where you will place your grid. Your main consideration should be finding a place where it is unlikely to be disturbed. You can then decide what size grid will fit in that space and collect enough crystals to match the space available. Then, just before you start, cleanse all the crystals you want to use (see pages 10–11).

BUILDING AND ACTIVATING YOUR GRID

Thinking of the outcome you want, do the following:

1. Start building the grid, adding the crystals in this order:
   - 1 × centre stone (the largest stone, placed in the centre of the grid to direct its energy up into the Universe);
   - 6 × desire stones, chosen to match the theme of the grid and arranged in a hexagon around the centre stone;
   - 6 × way stones, positioned between the centre stone and the desire stones to direct energy to the centre of the grid. Way stones are usually either Clear Quartz or the same crystal as the desire stones; more Clear Quartz points can be added in order to amplify and steer the energy of the grid.

2. To activate your grid, touch the centre stone with your finger.

3. Touch one of the surrounding stones.

4. Go back and touch the centre stone again.

5. Touch the next surrounding stone.

6. Keep doing this until you have touched all the stones.

7. Keep your crystal grid until you have met your intention or you can see it is getting closer and you want to create a new grid more specific to your changing situation.

8. Mindfully thank the grid, take it down and cleanse the crystals.

CRYSTAL ELIXIRS

Crystal elixirs are the perfect way to internalize a crystal's energies. An elixir is water endowed with the vibration of a crystal and is particularly good for physical ailments and emotional support. Our emotional body is connected to the Water element, so it makes sense to charge water with healing properties to aid our mental health.

Placing a crystal into water to create an elixir is called the *direct method*. This technique isn't suitable for all crystals, as some leave residue in the water, while others are harmful if consumed. In addition, some crystals will rust or break down in water. To avoid these issues, I recommend you only create *indirect method* elixirs. This involves placing the crystal next to a glass of water, rather than in it. As everything is energy, the crystal's vibration will still reach the water and program it without any of the worries involved with the direct method.

MAKING CRYSTAL ELIXIRS

1. Cleanse your crystal (see pages 10–11) and place it next to a drinking glass.
2. Pour the drinking water into the glass.
3. Leave them together for a minimum of 20 minutes.
4. Now drink the water.

CRYSTAL SHAPES

The following is a brief guide to the properties and symbolism of the different shapes I mention in this book.

Raw
The natural formation, perfect for display

Clusters
Support community

Tumbles, nuggets
Polished small crystals, ideal to carry

Chips
Polished crystals, smaller than tumbles. Often used in ritual or for decoration

Freeform
Cut to enhance the crystal's natural features

Slab
A slice of a crystal that creates a natural display base for other items

Towers, points
Direct energy up into the Universe

Double termination
Dispels stagnant energy

Palm stones, worry stones
Calm, comfort and help to deepen meditation

Spheres
Cultivate feminine energy

Cubes
Cultivate masculine energy

Pyramids
Represent duality

Egg shapes
Support new beginnings, birth and motherhood

Hearts
Support relationships and loving kindness towards ourselves and others

Flames
Symbolize aspects of the Fire element

Skulls, alien skulls
When a crystal takes on human form, we can build a greater relationship with it

Sacred geometry sets, merkabahs
Embrace the mathematics of nature, enhancing the energies of the crystals

Talisman shapes, including angels, moons, water droplets and leaves
Symbolize the character the shape represents

Wands
Command and direct energy

Mirror
A tool for the psychic skill of scrying

Bowls
Hold items so they can take on the crystal's energies

Jewellery
Allows us to wear crystals on the body. Crystals faceted or shaped for jewellery are called cabochons

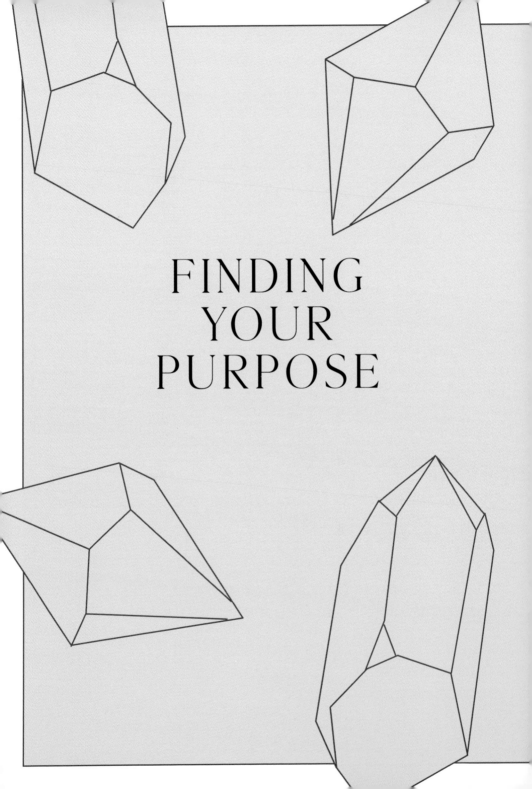

FINDING
YOUR
PURPOSE

On page 15 I explained that most people start focusing on self-development and then progress onto spiritual development.

Self-development can be broken down into physical and emotional goals. In essence, these are all about making personal choices that will help us achieve greater levels of happiness. Physical goals focus on improving our health and supporting our physical body, while emotional goals look at aiding our mental health and identifying any fears, limiting beliefs or past trauma that could be holding us back.

Spiritual development is closely connected to our soul purpose and might include travel aspirations and career goals as well as our ideal home life and hobbies. We often want to prioritize these spiritual goals but in reality we need to focus on all three. Imagine a wise old oak tree: it needs strong, wide-reaching roots to be able to grow tall. In other words, supporting your physical and emotional health will make it easier for you to achieve your spiritual goals.

If you feel your goal is going to take longer than three months to complete, try to split it up into smaller segments. The different stages of a larger goal require different energies, so if you divide the goal up, you can check in at each stage and make sure you have the right crystal for that part of it.

Once you have put the steps in place for a healthy body, your improved health will support the work you need to do to complete other goals. Therefore, I'm going to suggest you start with a physical goal.

The crystal plan process for a physical goal is the easiest to work through. So starting here allows me to quickly show you the full process.

Physical Purpose

We start by exploring what your current physical purpose might be. This represents any goals you have relating to your physical body and overall health and would include identifying the specific crystal needed to support any ailments you might have. Perhaps you are also dreaming of taking up an activity that requires a greater amount of physical strength and flexibility; or maybe you want to start a family, so your goal would be to find the perfect fertility support crystal.

HOW THE ENERGY BODY SUPPORTS THE PHYSICAL BODY

When I first started studying spiritual and holistic health in my early twenties, one particularly inspirational teacher explained to us how we in the West regularly wait until we have clear signs of bad health before tackling it. On one level this makes complete sense: we start to feel unwell, so we act to help ourselves. What many of us are not taught but ancient cultures intuitively knew is that it is possible to act much sooner.

If you imagine the chakras as a gateway between the energetic and the physical body, you can see that keeping them unblocked will alleviate any energy build-up that our body might take on. Even the word disease, literally 'dis-ease', describes this imbalance of energy.

Therefore, when choosing physical goals I would recommend seeing your progression in two stages. Stage one would involve supporting anything that might have already manifested in the physical body so you can relieve any energy that has built up. Then, when it feels right to do so, you can move to stage two and consider creating goals that help you strive for optimal health.

With that in mind, before we can choose the perfect crystal for your current physical needs, we must identify the kind of support you would like.

FIND YOUR PHYSICAL GOAL

To help determine your physical goals, try the journaling prompts below. Work through the questions one by one. Split your physical goals into two stages, as suggested on the previous page, and journal on both points.

JOURNAL PROMPTS

1. What changes to your diet do you feel would make the biggest impact?

2. Consider how changing your level of physical exercise would improve your overall health, what those changes could be and how they might make you feel. (Only consider activities you would enjoy doing.)

3. a: Are there any physical activities you can't currently do but you would like to be able to do?

   b: If yes, consider what has stopped you already implementing this.

4. Looking at your answers to the previous questions, are there any changes you would like to make that feel particularly hard? Consider what you could do to make this easier.

WHAT IS YOUR GOAL?

Hopefully the journal prompts have given you ideas for potential goals. Now choose the one that you feel the most eager to complete. That eagerness will keep you motivated. You might also need to consider what part of the body needs supporting. For example, if your goal is to run 10km (6 miles), is your focus on increasing your stamina, the strength in your legs, or your back, heart or lung capacity? Now you have your main goal, sum it up in a short sentence that includes a clear measurable outcome so that you will know when you have achieved it.

PHYSICAL PURPOSE AND THE CHAKRAS

Having identified your goal, look for the chakra that matches the theme of your goal on the table overleaf. The colour that relates to it will be the colour of the crystal you need to select in the Choosing Your Crystals chapter (see pages 46–55).

Use this table to find the chakra that best supports the area of the body that relates to your goal. Then look for the crystal colour you need. If there is more than one relevant chakra, choose the one located highest up the table.

CHAKRA	PHYSICAL AREAS RELATED TO EACH CHAKRA	LOCATIONS, AREAS AND AILMENTS RELATED TO EACH CHAKRA
Root chakra	Pubic bone to toes (includes male genitals)	Bones, skin, teeth, bowel, anus, large intestine, male genitals * Arthritis, haemorrhoids, constipation, sciatica, eating disorders, weight problems, male reproductive disorders and sexual dysfunction, frequent illness and deficiencies of various kinds
Sacral chakra	Belly button to pubic bone (includes female genitals)	Womb, female genitals, kidneys, bladder, lower back * Flexibility, menstrual difficulties, female reproductive disorders and sexual dysfunction
Solar plexus chakra	Ribcage down to top of belly button	Digestive system, muscles * Vitality, digestive disorders, ulcers, hypoglycaemia, diabetes, muscle spasms and disorders, chronic fatigue, hypertension, stomach disorders, pancreas, gallbladder and liver
Heart chakra	Collarbone to ribcage (includes arms)	Heart, lungs, breasts, hands and arms, circulatory and respiratory systems * Heart and lung disease, circulation problems, high blood pressure, asthma and immune system deficiencies
Throat chakra	Lower jaw, mouth and ears, down to collarbone	Ears, mouth and neck * Disorders of the throat, ears, voice and neck, tightness of jaw and toxicity
Third eye chakra	Crown of head, down to upper jaw (includes eyes)	Eyes, mind * Headaches and vision problems
Crown chakra	Crown of head	Cerebral cortex and the central nervous system * Migraines, foggy head, brain disorders and trauma and genetic and life-threatening disorders

GLANDS	SENSE	CRYSTAL COLOUR
Adrenals	Smell	Red, black, brown, metallic and earthy colours
Ovaries and testicles (because of their location, the testicles are associated with this sacral chakra, although male reproductive health is usually covered by the root chakra)	Taste	Orange
Pancreas and adrenals	Sight	Yellow
Thymus	Touch	Pink and green
Thyroid and parathyroid	Hearing	Blue
Pineal	Mind – intuitive abilities	Purple
Pituitary	No attributed sense	White and transparent

Emotional Purpose

By now you are probably aware how important our energy body is and how caring for it mindfully can be beneficial in multiple ways. But how can you gauge the state of your energy body and its frequency?

Our emotions are a direct result of our energy levels. When our energies are high, we feel joy and happiness. When they are low, so too are our emotions. The lower the emotions, the more stuck and out of alignment with our soul purpose we become.

All emotions exist on a scale. The lowest, such as shame and guilt, are debilitating and leave us feeling energetically stuck. As we move up the scale, our emotions become more dynamic, giving us the mental space to improve our current experience, until we get to the middle of the scale, which is neutrality. From there we start going into the higher, more invigorating emotions, such as eagerness, empowerment and joy.

In essence, our emotions control our ability to achieve any goals, so we need to be in a positive emotional state to succeed in all areas of our lives.

Limiting beliefs, fears and blocks are also ways in which our emotions and mental health can hinder our growth. Often these beliefs come from events that happened to us when we were very young, so we might not remember the cause. They hide in our subconscious mind, playing out in different areas of our life. For example, a child might have taken on the belief that *they are not good enough*. Now as an adult that person might self-sabotage the opportunity for a promotion at work, allowing their subconscious to play out the belief. And all of this can be happening without our being aware of it.

When working with crystals, we don't need to know the cause of a negative thought pattern. Instead, we want to find a crystal with the energy to support us and use it to raise our vibration above that belief or mental block. The same applies when using crystals to improve our emotional state. We use the crystals to increase our frequency, and at the same time our emotions can improve too.

FIND YOUR EMOTIONAL GOAL

An emotional purpose goal (or emotional goal for short) looks at raising our vibration to improve our emotional state and heal old limiting beliefs, fears and anxieties so we can cultivate healthier thought patterns. While brain health fits into the physical goals section, anything to do with mental health fits into the emotional category, so when I use the phrase 'emotional' goals, I'm also referring to mental health.

When picking an emotional goal there are two categories you can look at:

1. Emotions or beliefs that are holding you back and need healing.
2. Emotions or characteristics that you would like to enhance or bring into your life to support you.

For example, it would benefit you to heal imposter syndrome, anxieties or financial blocks (first category), but it might also be useful if you could speak with more empathy or feel more confident (second category).

Your emotions and beliefs affect all areas of your life, so even when you focus on a physical or soul-aligned goal you might see some negative thought patterns appearing. When they do, it's worth coming back to this page, to find a crystal to work on those thoughts so you can make more progress towards your main goal.

JOURNAL PROMPTS

The best way to pinpoint the emotional goal you want to focus on is to take a timeout from everyday life, surround yourself with your favourite things and start journaling so you can discover what will be the best support for you.

Below is a series of journal prompts. Try to work through them all. Don't forget to sit with each question for as long as possible. The longer you write, the more insights will come. I suggest journaling on both the categories of emotional goals mentioned on the previous page, and consider what improvements you would like to make.

1. What are your fears?
2. Is there anything holding you back right now from achieving a goal?
3. Can you see the same relationship patterns playing out again and again in your life?
4. What characteristics do you admire in other people?
5. When you achieve this goal, what will your reward be?

WHAT IS YOUR GOAL?

Now looking at your journaling work. Take your time to highlight potential goals, especially if you have written about the same thing more than once. Remember, it is also worth looking to see if there are any specific areas that, if resolved, would heal other areas at the same time.

Once you've considered everything, it's time to choose your emotional goal. Make sure it's something that motivates you, that you feel excited to work on. Write that goal as a short sentence, giving a time frame and a clear outcome so you will know when you've achieved it.

EMOTIONAL PURPOSE AND THE CHAKRAS

Now you know your goal, you can pinpoint the chakra that correlates with it to find the colour of crystal you need.

For each of the three goal themes – physical, emotional and soul-aligned – the way we read the chakras changes. This time we read them from the bottom (the root chakra) up. This upwards energy flow is called the *current of liberation* and follows the order in which the chakras open as we grow and develop.

A newborn baby has only the root chakra open. This chakra represents our most fundamental needs: food, safety, protection and shelter.

As we develop and grow throughout childhood and into adulthood, the chakras open one by one. Each has its own themes which correlate with lessons the child will be going through at that time.

Once all the chakras are open, a big or small trauma might affect the energy flow to one of them. If an event has triggered the flight part of our protective 'fight or flight' reaction, the chakra relating to that theme might become *underactive*, as it's lacking energy. In contrast, if fight is triggered, more energy goes to that chakra, meaning it might become *overactive*.

It's important to note that these traumas can be anything from a major life-changing event to a small trip or fall or a moment of embarrassment we would have forgotten about that same day. Therefore, it's best not to focus too much on the cause but instead help release the energy around it so it's no longer affecting us.

Overleaf is a table showing all of the chakras, the developmental stage at which they open and the traits of a perfectly balanced chakra and an underactive chakra. You are looking for the chakra that correlates with your goal. When you find it, make a note of its colour, so that you know the colour of the crystal you need to select in the Choosing Your Crystals chapter (see pages 46–55).

Use this table to find where your specific emotional block or limiting belief is held, then look for the colour of the crystal that will support you. If there is more than one relevant chakra, choose the one located highest up the table.

CHAKRA	BALANCED CHAKRA TRAITS
Root chakra	Enjoys and trusts life, is safe, secure, stable, prosperous, comfortable in body, grounded, does not mind change
Sacral chakra	Emotionally intelligent, passionate, has a healthy libido, healthy relationships with others and self, good boundaries, creative, graceful movement
Solar plexus chakra	Confident, responsible, reliable, independent, plenty of vitality, spontaneous, sense of humour, personal power, warmth, drive
Heart chakra	Peaceful, balanced, loving, compassionate, empathetic, tolerant, altruistic, forgiving
Throat chakra	Confident and able communicator, expressive, good listener, good sense of timing and rhythm
Third eye chakra	Imaginative, intuitive, perceptive, good memory, assimilates information, clear thoughts and vision, able to see beyond the physical
Crown chakra	Strong faith, spiritually connected, feels universal love and consciousness, intelligent, open-minded, questioning, able to receive intuitive guidance as a thought or idea, is aware, wise and understanding

UNDERACTIVE CHAKRA TRAITS	CRYSTAL COLOUR
Fearful, anxious, restless, unable to relax, has poor boundaries, financial difficulties, disorganized, poor discipline, disconnected from the body, neglects self, not grounded	Red, black, brown, metallic and earthy colours
Poor social skills, lack of creativity or passion, unhealthy relationships, co-dependency, negative attachment, excessive boundaries, low libido, fear of sex or intimacy, sexual trauma, addiction	Orange
Low self-esteem, feels powerless, poor self-discipline, easily manipulated, unreliable, suffers from inferiority complex or imposter syndrome, cold and low energy	Yellow
Heartbroken, lacks empathy, feels bitter, rejected, finds it hard to love unconditionally, filled with hate, anti-social, isolated, intolerant	Pink and green
Can't express self or speak out, feels misunderstood, secretive, not a good listener, low voice, shy, tone deaf and poor rhythm	Blue
Poor imagination, memory and judgement. In denial, holds polarized views, insensitive, can't see beyond the physical	Purple
Critical of spirituality, has rigid belief systems, weak faith, depression, apathy, learning difficulties, anger at the Divine, loneliness	White and transparent

Soul Purpose

Having become familiar with the crystal plan process, you may already have chosen a crystal for a physical or emotional goal. Now it's time to find the crystal that will help you achieve your soul-aligned goals. These are goals that are directly connected to your soul purpose: the experiences, lessons and achievements your soul planned for you to learn.

It was important to start with the other goals, in order to create a good physical and emotional foundation from which to strive for these big, aspirational goals.

Unlike our physical and emotional goals that focus on healing and making changes, soul purpose goals are about realizing who we are at the deepest level.

Many people's soul purpose matches their childhood dreams or a hobby that brought them joy and they may be able to turn this into a career. For others, their soul purpose is presented to them later in life as something they or a loved one need to overcome, a series of difficult events that has changed their life dramatically. It could be anything from a bereavement or illness to fostering a child, emigrating, starting a new career or becoming an activist for a cause they believe in deeply. This experience motivates them to support others going through the same thing.

We all have a special way of doing things that is unique to us, something we might overlook, but that our friends will know to be our superpower. The skills we display might not be career related; instead they probably bring us a lot of joy and come naturally to us. These are the skills that will help us achieve our soul purpose.

FIND YOUR SOUL GOAL

At this point you might have a number of potential soul purpose goals. That is brilliant. In my opinion, we only dream of things that we know on some level we can achieve – so let's get you working through them all. Right now, though, it's time to decide where to start.

Overleaf are some journal prompts aimed at helping you consider the different things you could focus on, so you can refine them to one goal.

As always, please take as long as you can to answer each question. The obvious answers always come first, before the more profound information. You might even want to take a few days to compile your answers to see if any extra insights come through.

JOURNAL PROMPTS

1. What brings you joy?
2. If your loved ones were to describe you and your best skills, what would they say?
3. What do people ask you for support with?
4. What did you love doing as a child?
5. If you went to a psychic to find out what your soul purpose was, what do you think they would say?
6. How are you going to reward yourself for achieving this goal?

WHAT IS YOUR GOAL?

Now it's time to pinpoint that first goal. Looking at what you have written, what stands out? Are there any patterns? What would you like to explore or test out? Unlike the other goals that most likely have a clear outcome, a goal relating to your soul purpose will honour your progression through life. It might be about launching a new business, but it might also be about exploring and trying out new things.

So that you don't feel overwhelmed by this goal, I'm going to ask again that you focus on something that can be achieved in three months or less. I'd also like it to have a measurable end point, so you will know when you have achieved it and when it's time to celebrate.

Once you have done that, it's time to look at the chakras so you can see what colours you need.

SOUL PURPOSE AND THE CHAKRAS

This time we read the chakras top to bottom (crown to root chakra). This downwards flow of energy is called the *current of manifestation* and it reflects how the creative process works.

The higher chakras, with their more etheric energies (the energies that deal with the unseen, our emotional energy and our higher self rather than the physical body), focus on the idea and inspiration behind a new project. Then, as we start to plan and create, the energies move down through the chakras, ending with the densest energy at the root chakra. This represents the end of a project, when we have a final 'physical thing' we can present to the world.

The table overleaf shows how the current of manifestation supports a new project and highlights the blocks or setbacks that can happen along the way. As you read I want you to consider what part of the manifestation/creative process you find hard and what chakra that relates to. In your past experiences, what has slowed down a project or stopped you progressing altogether?

Some of the issues I've listed on the table overleaf are negative thought patterns as mentioned in the emotional purpose section (see page 34). In that section we were looking at supporting emotions in general. Here we are looking for negative thought patterns that directly affect our soul purpose goals. In these cases it does not matter which process we use: the outcome and the colour we need will be the same.

Once you pinpoint the chakra, note the colour(s) connected to it and then move on to the Choosing Your Crystals chapter (see pages 46–55).

Use this table to identify the chakra whose traits you see in yourself. Then look for the crystal colour that relates to that chakra. If there is more than one relevant chakra, choose the one located highest up the table.

CHAKRA	BALANCED CHAKRA TRAITS
Crown chakra	We start here as a new project begins with a spark of inspiration entering through the crown chakra and appearing as an idea in the third eye. This is the most energetic part of the manifestation process and requires that our crown chakra be fully open for us to be able to receive new ideas.
Third eye chakra	When we receive an idea, our third eye turns it into a thought. People with a very open crown chakra will receive so many ideas that it might be hard for them to identify the ones they want to progress.
Throat chakra	Once we have an idea that we want to progress, we start problem-solving each step to consider how realistic the idea is. These internal conversations engage the throat chakra. They then progress to external conversations with our loved ones.
Heart chakra	As we tell people about our ideas, the excitement inside us builds and the energy moves downwards to the heart. At this stage we literally fall in love with an idea and want it to be part of our life.
Solar plexus chakra	When an idea reaches the solar plexus it's time to start creating. This marks the first day of setting up that new business, starting that new course or writing that book.
Sacral chakra	Once we have started a project and the momentum has begun we move into the orange energy of the sacral chakra. This is the willpower and perseverance energy that helps us to get over that finishing line.
Root chakra	This marks the end of a project, when we have something physical we can show other people.

UNDERACTIVE CHAKRA TRAITS	CRYSTAL COLOUR
If you feel you don't have any direction or don't receive inspiration, focusing on balancing the crown chakra will help this process begin.	White and transparent
You may feel overwhelmed with ideas and not progress any of them or you start one idea and wish you had done another. In these circumstances, you need stronger third eye energy to strengthen the energy of good ideas or to make the perfect idea to stand out: more purple energy will be good for you.	Purple
If you find you are mulling over ideas a lot, telling people about your dreams but never doing much about them, you need more throat chakra blue. An increase in throat chakra energy means you stop speaking your dreams and start speaking your truth. Once this happens, the *law of attraction* is engaged and the Universe will help you to manifest.	Blue
If you do fall in love with an idea but within weeks your attention has moved onto something else, you need more pink or green heart chakra energy. This really ignites that passion, encouraging you to progress an idea further.	Pink and green
Your solar plexus gives you the confidence and vitality to begin a project, but it can easily be stifled by imposter syndrome or feelings of *I'm not good enough*. To overcome anything like this, more yellow energy is needed.	Yellow
If you feel you start projects but then lose interest and want to take a break or do something else, more orange energy will keep you focused.	Orange
It's a big moment and one many will shy away from, rather than celebrate. Consider the artist who would never hang their work on the wall or the entrepreneur who builds a business but sells it as soon as it launches. If you feel you don't enjoy telling people about your finished projects or achievements, then more root chakra colours will be a good support.	Red, black, brown, metallic and earthy colours

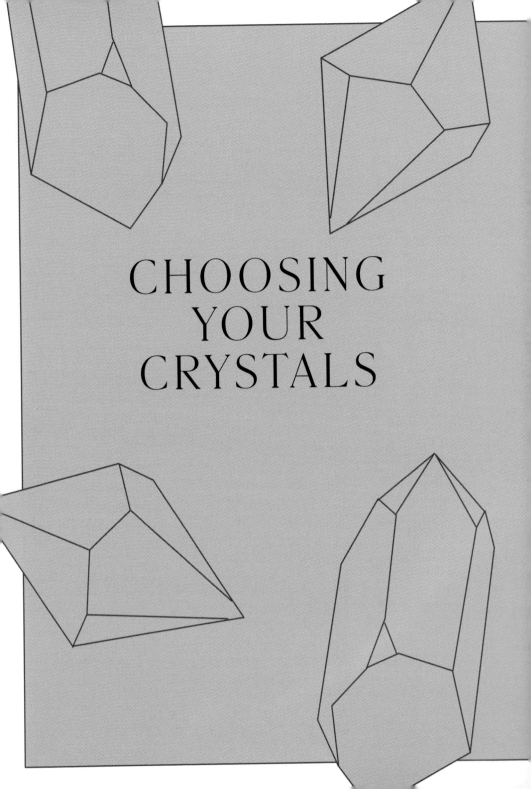

CHOOSING
YOUR
CRYSTALS

At this point you have identified your goals and know the colour frequency that best supports them. Now you can use that information to help you choose the ideal crystals for your current needs.

Up until this moment you have used logical, analytical, left-brain skills. These are perfect for identifying the goals you want to pursue and the colours you need to support them. Now you are ready to switch things up and bring in the right brain and its intuitive abilities.

Most of the time, the underlying cause of any long-term issue is hidden in our subconscious mind, which is directly connected to our right brain. We always want to make sure we are finding crystals to heal at that deep level, as it allows us to focus on the initial belief, issue or event which is at the root of the problem.

When we heal that original layer, we will also be working on any other layers of physical, emotional or spiritual trauma that reinforce the original event. We might think we logically know the cause of an issue, but the true cause could be hidden away in our subconscious. Therefore, if we use only the left brain to choose the crystals, we might not be going deep enough. Selecting crystals using our intuition, our right brain, will ensure we are addressing the core issues.

As you select the crystals for your crystal plan, I would recommend picking one for all the other colours as well. That will help you create your own personalised chakra set that best suits your energies and current needs. A chakra set is made up of seven crystals that match the colours of the seven major chakras. You can then head to page 18 to learn how to use all seven in a full chakra balance.

Using Intuition to Choose a Crystal

We are attracted to crystals whose frequency will best support us. When we go into a crystal shop and one crystal stands out, that is our intuition's way of highlighting what we need. So all we need to do is choose the crystal we love the most within the colour scheme we have identified engaging our intuition.

INTUITION PRACTICE

There are two ways to choose crystals: visually or energetically. On pages 49–55 you will find a page devoted to each of the seven main chakras and its relevant colour(s), featuring a selection of popular crystals for that chakra. Find the relevant page for the chakra you need and try choosing the crystal that you are drawn to. Practise both the following techniques.

TECHNIQUE ONE: VISUAL SELECTION

1. Close your eyes and take some deep breaths to calm your mind.

2. Recall your intention – to choose your ideal crystal from those available.

3. Look at the image. The crystal you look at first is the right one for you.

TECHNIQUE TWO: ENERGY SELECTION

1. Take some deep breaths to calm the mind.

2. Recall your intention – to choose your ideal crystal from those available.

3. Look at each crystal image while you hover the palm of your hand a few inches above the page. The right crystal for you will create a sensation in your body, normally in the palm. You might feel chilly, get goosebumps or feel tingling or sweating in your palms.

Once you've worked out which technique works best for you, select your crystal then go to pages 56–207 to learn more about your chosen crystals, their common properties and how to work with them.

 ROOT CHAKRA CRYSTALS

RED, BLACK, BROWN, METALLIC AND EARTHY

Arfvedsonite

Black Moonstone

Black Obsidian

Black Tourmaline

Bloodstone

Fire Opal

Fire Quartz

Garnet

Petrified Wood

Pyrite

Red Aragonite

Red Jasper

Smoky Quartz

SACRAL CHAKRA CRYSTALS

ORANGE

Carnelian

Copper

Orange Calcite

Peach Moonstone

Stilbite

Sunstone

Tangerine Quartz

Vanadinite

SOLAR PLEXUS CHAKRA CRYSTALS

YELLOW

Amber

Citrine

Gold

Golden Healer

Golden Tiger's Eye

Golden Topaz

Gold Rutilated Quartz

Honey Calcite

Libyan Desert Glass

Muscovite Mica

Sulphur

PINK AND GREEN

Amazonite

Botswana Agate

Emerald

Flower Agate

Green Aventurine

Green Jade

Malachite

Moldavite

Morganite

Moss Agate

Peridot

Rose Quartz

Watermelon
Tourmaline

BLUE

Angelite

Aquamarine

Blue Chalcedony

Blue Kyanite

Blue Lace Agate

Blue Topaz

Chrysocolla

Labradorite

Larimar

Sodalite

Tanzanite

Turquoise

THIRD EYE CHAKRA CRYSTALS

PURPLE

Amethyst

Ametrine

Charoite

Lithium Quartz

Purple Fluorite

Spirit Quartz

Sugilite

CROWN CHAKRA CRYSTALS

WHITE AND TRANSPARENT

Apophyllite

Clear Quartz

Elestial Quartz

Goddess Stone

Herkimer Diamond

Howlite

Limestone

Scolecite

Selenite

Tourmalated
Quartz

White Opal

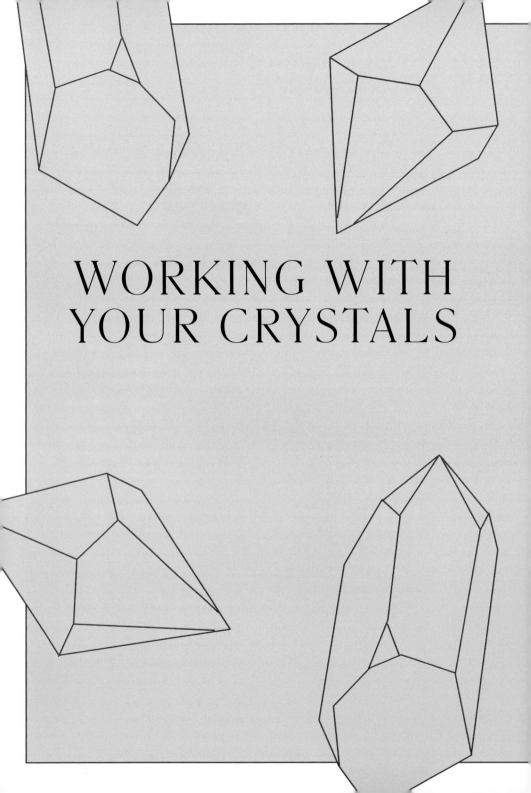

WORKING WITH
YOUR CRYSTALS

By this stage, your crystal plan is in place. You have identified your goals and selected the ideal crystals to support them. Now it's time to learn about those crystals.

Depending on whether you chose a crystal for a physical, emotional or soul-aligned goal, there will be 'best practice' ways to work with it. I have presented three techniques, one for each goal theme. These are inspired by the main properties of that crystal and common reasons we are drawn to its energy.

Sometimes you might not resonate with the properties of a crystal I've chosen to talk about, because all of our experiences are individual and personal to us. Nevertheless, please try each technique, as they represent the best way to work with that crystal and its energies to give you and your plan optimal support. Working with the crystal is more important than pinpointing exactly what property attracted you to it.

Over time, trying these techniques, along with the standard techniques I outlined on pages 16–27, will deepen your connection and help you understand the different ways you can use your crystal as an energy tool.

ARFVEDSONITE

GALACTIC SUPPORT

Arfvedsonite is a very rare mineral composed of potassium, iron, titanium, manganese, sodium and silicate. It forms as a fine-bladed crystal that when polished looks like galaxies, giving us a clue as to its properties. It has a surprisingly etheric energy for a root chakra crystal. Even though it offers practical support for the physical world, being drawn to this crystal may indicate that you feel more connected to the energetic body than the physical.

Physical: Those who have a strong connection to the galaxies can have an unhealthy relationship with the physical body. They might not prioritize their physical health. If this resonates with you, try the following to integrate your energies into the physical body.

STARSEED EMBODIMENT

1. Source an Arfvedsonite point for the physical body, a green crystal for the emotional body and a white crystal for the spiritual body.
2. Create a large triangle with your three crystal points facing inwards.
3. Lie in that triangle several times a week for 10–20 minutes. As you do this, have the intention that you are integrating all aspects of yourself.

Emotional: Selecting Arfvedsonite for emotional support suggests you might need to meet like-minded people who understand and can support you. To attract these people, team up Arfvedsonite with Muscovite Mica (the crystal for cultivating a community – see page 118) and create a crystal grid with the intention of attracting new people into your life (see page 25).

Soul: Choosing Arfvedsonite suggests you have innate spiritual skills with a galactic theme that you are ready to explore. Keep your crystal by your bedside as you sleep, so you can receive guidance relating to these new skills.

Additional properties: Expands consciousness, strengthens the stellar gateway chakra (see page 136), connects the Earth star chakra (see page 140) with the soul star chakra (see page 136)

Additional techniques: Meditate with Arfvedsonite in order to connect to your galactic guides.

Suggested shapes: Points, skulls, alien skulls, merkaba, palms, tumbles

Source: The USA, Canada, Greenland, Russia

BLACK MOONSTONE

SHADOW WORK

Black Moonstone asks us to look deep inside ourselves and do *shadow work*. This refers to the parts of us hidden in our subconscious mind that we have repressed. They could include characteristics that society says are bad, as well as shame, guilt, deception and secret fears.

Physical and Emotional: Selecting Black Moonstone as your physical or emotional support suggests the body would like the opportunity to release anything that could be building up. Try sitting or lying down and placing the crystal over your heart. Take a few deep breaths to relax the body and ask your heart *what needs clearing.* When you receive an answer, move the crystal to that spot and breathe into that area. Then, ask: *What emotion is there and what does it want to tell me?* Often the energy starts to release once that information is shared. Keep holding the crystal over that spot until you instinctively feel that healing has happened. You might need two or three sessions to fully clear an energy.

Soul: Selecting Black Moonstone to support soul-aligned goals suggests that working on those shadows will clear out old energies, helping your goals to come to fruition.

1. Start by writing down all the things you might feel are aspects of your shadow side. Make sure you also consider inherited behaviours you might have received from other people.

2. Pinpoint the ones that, if resolved, could impact your life the most.

3. Choose one or two and make a list of the lessons those particular events or emotions have given you or the positive outcomes that might happen if you engage that emotion.

4. Burn the list to release those emotions and place your Black Moonstone over the ashes to represent the healing of any residual energy that remains.

Additional properties: Matriarchal, dealing with past-life witch-wound healing (that is, memories of being persecuted, which can show up in the form of nightmares and fears), guiding us through the cycles of life and connecting to the Moon

Additional techniques: Create a Black Moonstone crystal grid (see page 25) under the Full Moon to facilitate deep healing.

Suggested shapes: Palms, hearts, spheres, moons, talisman shapes

Source: Madagascar

BLACK OBSIDIAN

also called Volcanic Glass, Glassy Lava

PROTECTION

Within crystal therapy all black crystals are classed as having protective energies. Protection is one of the main themes of the root chakra and is a fundamental need for any human being. To be able to develop and grow we first need to feel safe.

Physical: To support all aspects of the root chakra, for three minutes each day place a crystal specimen on either side of your hips. Do this for at least two weeks.

Emotional: A common negative thought pattern that gets stuck in the root chakra is *I'm not safe.* This can play out in all areas of life and often stops us from stepping out of our comfort zone to try new things. Subtle beliefs such as this can easily be held in our energy body.

To release these subconscious beliefs and to support your subtle body, place five or six crystals in a circle around your body. That way it's connected to your auric field. Lie in the centre for 15–20 minutes once a week.

Soul: If you feel drained after spending time with specific people or visiting specific places it can help you to learn to protect your energies. The process of cord cutting stops your energies being drained and returns them to you.

1. Close your eyes, then in your mind's eye imagine a cord connecting you to the person or location that might have drained your energy.
2. Pass your Black Obsidian through the cord with the intention that the crystal is cutting the cord.
3. Now imagine half of the cord's energy returning to you and the other half going back to the cause of the energy drain.
4. Before opening your eyes, imagine replacing the cord with white light.

Additional properties: Grounding, invoking fast change and the Fire element, clearing meridian lines

Additional techniques: Place a specimen by the front door so that only positive energies can enter the home.

Suggested shapes: Arrows, flames, mirrors, moons, double terminated points

Source: Worldwide, in areas that have seen volcanic activity

BLACK TOURMALINE

GROUNDING

Black Tourmaline has some of the most grounding and reassuring energies I've experienced from the crystal kingdom. Its energies are subtle, so you might not feel them, but you will definitely feel the results of working with them.

Physical: Place a collection of small crystal specimens in a line travelling all the way down your legs, from your hips to your toes. This energetically strengthens the skeletal system and lower torso.

Emotional: If you selected Black Tourmaline for an emotional goal, it could be that you have an underlying belief around the theme *I'm not safe*. Normally these beliefs develop when we are very young (under two years old) and can happen for all kinds of reasons, some less obvious than others. For example, if a caregiver receives a shock when holding us, it can trigger the subconscious to believe that life isn't safe.

To give the subconscious space to release this kind of belief, carry Black Tourmaline with you as often as possible.

Soul: Some people feel more of a connection to their energy body than to their physical one. To reconnect to your physical body, lie down and place a large Black Tourmaline specimen under each foot, ideally with its rods facing away from the body. While having the intention to welcome your energies fully back into the body, relax and focus on your breath.

Additional properties: Protection, invoking the Earth element

Additional techniques: Place a specimen of Black Tourmaline in the four corners of the home for protection.

Suggested shapes: Raw, chips, palms, towers

Source: Brazil, Africa, Pakistan, the USA

BLOODSTONE *also called Heliotrope*

ANCESTRAL HEALING

It's no surprise that Bloodstone supports the cardiovascular system, specifically blood health. The name also speaks of our genetic 'bloodline', making this the perfect crystal for ancestral and inter-generational healing.

Physical: To support blood health and offer it an energetic detox, either wear Bloodstone jewellery or create an elixir (see page 26) to use daily for at least a week. Ideally, take some of your elixir after your evening meal, allowing it to work its magic as you sleep.

Emotional: Selecting Bloodstone to support your emotional goals indicates that exploring recent or ancient *generational trauma*, which can be handed down via learned behaviour, historic events and genetics, will aid your progress.

GENERATIONAL TRAUMA RITUAL

1. At least one day before you carry out the ritual, place your Bloodstone in a glass and add 3 pinches of 2 or more of the following: lavender, mugwort, rosebuds, sage or myrrh. Then leave it in the sunshine.
2. Holding a charcoal tablet with some tongs, set light to it and place it somewhere it can burn safely.
3. Take the Bloodstone out of the glass and thank it.
4. Pour the herbs over the charcoal so that they start to burn.
5. While you watch the smoke rising, contemplate how it symbolizes the energies being released so the healing can begin.

Soul: Selecting Bloodstone for spiritual work suggests that, with practice, you will be able to receive messages from your ancestors. Source a Bloodstone necklace and, when you need guidance, hold the charm, close your eyes and ask a question. Take a breath and allow the answer to come to you.

Additional properties: Balancing blood sugars, letting down your defences, overcoming loneliness

Additional techniques: Wear Bloodstone to experience more compassion in everyday situations.

Suggested shapes: Jewellery, tumbles, hearts

Source: India, China, Brazil, Australia, the USA

FIRE OPAL

PROSPERITY

On page 43 I explained the downwards flow of manifestation energy that goes through the chakras. The flash of colour that appears on a Fire Opal holds all the colours of the rainbow, offering up its energies to keep that flow of energy clear so our dreams can move through the chakras and into reality. That is why Fire Opal is known as a powerful prosperity crystal.

Physical: This is a really positive crystal to choose for your physical health. By selecting Fire Opal you are asking all the chakras and all the energies available to you to support the changes you want to make. For this reason I would suggest wearing a Fire Opal ring regularly for ongoing healing.

Emotional: All opals contain water, which symbolizes the emotional body and makes opal a brilliant support for emotional goals. We can find old emotional wounds trapped in all our chakras. Selecting Fire Opal suggests that healing work is needed on more than one chakra, so wearing it will help support each area.

Soul: Are you ready for a positive change? Fire Opal calls on the element of Fire to burn away anything that isn't serving you. It specifically focuses on the chakras, clearing any blocks that are preventing you from realizing your soul purpose.

Once a day for a week, use your Fire Opal to do a chakra balance (see page 18). Place your crystal over each chakra for two minutes. When you get to the crown, start working back down the body. At each stage imagine the Fire element burning away anything that's blocking that chakra.

Additional properties: Balancing, invoking the Fire element

Additional techniques: Take a crystal elixir to heal trapped emotions.

Suggested shapes: Jewellery, cabochons

Source: Mexico, Brazil, Australia, Ethiopia

ROOT CHAKRA CRYSTALS

FIRE QUARTZ *also called Hematite Quartz*

EMBRACING CHANGE

Fire Quartz contains the iron-based mineral hematite, which gives it its red colour. Its transparent appearance indicates etheric properties that are connected to our soul's development. The element of Fire is closely connected to our soul purpose because it is responsible for the *fire in our bellies* that is only satisfied when we are striving to achieve our biggest goals. When we are drawn to this crystal it indicates we are ready to embark on our soul purpose work.

Physical: When we work on our soul purpose, the joy it brings naturally raises our vibration. Our physical bodies can take time to become familiar with these energetic changes. Wearing Fire Quartz jewellery or using it to do a crystal layout in our auric field (see page 18) helps the physical body integrate these energies.

Emotional and Soul: Goals that relate to these themes often involve making changes in our life. Growth is always outside our comfort zone, so making change, big or small, is part of our soul's work.

Treat yourself to a piece of Fire Quartz jewellery that you can wear all the time. See it as a reminder of how proud you should be of yourself and of the big work you are doing. When those worries and fears come, thank your egoic mind for trying to keep you safe, hold your Fire Quartz jewellery and take that positive step forwards.

If you selected Fire Quartz specifically for spiritual support, this also indicates you would like some guidance in making positive changes. Do a chakra balance once a week (see page 18). Once you have put your seven chakra crystals in place, add your Fire Quartz specimen 1m (3ft) above your head so it's over the soul star chakra (the home of your soul's energy, see page 134). That way your chakras can pick up on any guidance your higher self would like to offer.

Additional properties: Passion for life, motivation, drive

Additional techniques: Place over the stomach to ignite the fire in the belly.

Suggested shapes: Jewellery, towers, flames

Source: The USA, Brazil, Madagascar

GARNET

BIRTHING

Semi-precious stones give off the most potent healing frequency of that crystal's colour. As a semi-precious stone, Garnet is a powerful root chakra crystal. It is one of the best for physical birth, and also the metaphysical birthing of new things.

Physical: Garnet is a well-known fertility crystal that can offer support for both males and females, from adolescence to old age. When used specifically for fertility work it is best kept in a trouser or coat pocket so that it is positioned near the genitals. You could even sew a crystal into the lining of a coat.

Emotional: Selecting Garnet for emotional support suggests potential birth trauma, a complicated pregnancy or miscarriage: this may be something you are afraid may happen, or it may already have happened to you, or to your mother or even to her mother. In these cases, it's time to cocoon yourself in a ball of love and compassion. The physical steps given above will help; for further support, follow the steps on page 144, using a Rose Quartz for self-care.

If you haven't gone through this kind of trauma yourself, choosing Garnet may indicate an inherited emotional wound, possibly a very old one. Crystal therapists may see this as a dense build-up in your energy field that, in my experience, shows up when it is ready to be released. To help with this, sip a Garnet elixir (see page 26) throughout the day for three days.

Soul: When you are drawn to Garnet for spiritual support, it is often because you deserve to be proud of your accomplishments, but instead you're shying away from showing your achievements to the world. Often our soul-aligned goals result in things we can talk about and show others. To support this, place a raw Garnet specimen in your workspace. That way its energy becomes connected to your project and your confidence levels build as you progress.

Additional properties: Fertility, craftsmanship, creative skills

Additional techniques: Place a specimen under the bed to enhance fertility and increase your sex drive.

Suggested shapes: Raw, palms, spheres, jewellery

Source: Brazil, India, Sri Lanka

PETRIFIED WOOD *also called Fossil Wood*

TRUST

Petrified Wood is created when a tree dies and starts to decay, allowing quartz crystal to collect in the alcoves that it creates. Over time, more of the tree dies and is replaced with quartz, until the remaining wood is preserved (also called petrified) in quartz.

All living trees and plants emanate their own unique frequency. When wood is encased in quartz, those energies are amplified to give a crystal that exudes natural, grounding energies.

Physical: Our physical health improves when we feel more connected to nature. To replicate this, lie down and place a crystal specimen under each foot. This brings your energies through the body to the feet so you feel more of a connection to the Earth.

Emotional: Many people hold the subconscious belief that *life isn't safe, the world isn't safe* or *I'm not safe*. When we connect to something as old as Petrified Wood (which is at least 5,000 years old), it exudes an energy of trust and reassurance that can only come from something that has existed for so long. Displaying a crystal specimen like that in your home can offer reassurance and resolve those fears.

Soul: Some people find life harsh and uncaring. If that resonates with you, reconnecting to your ancestral lineage can offer you greater levels of belonging and reassurance.

Petrified Wood also represents your family tree. To feel more connected to your ancestors, consider sourcing a slice of Petrified Wood you can use as a base to display photos of them on.

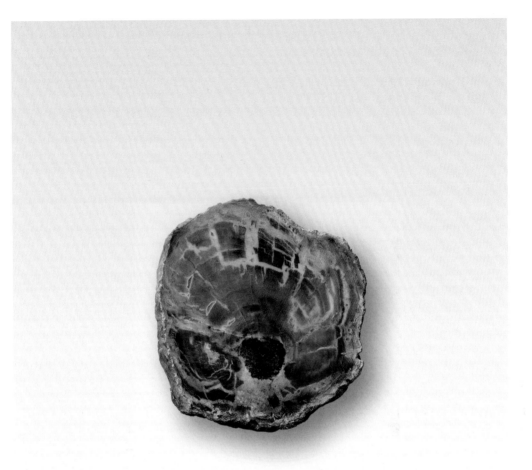

Additional properties: Grounding, connecting to the trees, forests and woods

Additional techniques: If you live in a built-up area, displaying Petrified Wood in your home will bring nature indoors.

Suggested shapes: Slabs, cubes, hearts, worry stones, palms

Source: The USA, Brazil, Madagascar

PYRITE *also called Fool's Gold*

FINANCIAL ABUNDANCE

Nineteenth-century miners confused 'fool's gold' with the real thing. Pyrite does not have the same value but is still connected to financial prosperity.

Physical: You may be drawn to Pyrite if your body is lacking something, as it helps the body to replenish. For this, try an indirect crystal elixir (see page 26).

Emotional: Choosing Pyrite for emotional support suggests you may have limiting beliefs that relate to self-worth and your relationship with money. The ritual below will help separate you from old behaviours and limiting beliefs.

PYRITE ABUNDANCE RITUAL

1. Place your Pyrite crystal about 1m (3ft) away from you. Imagine an energetic line between you and it. Where you stand represents your current situation. The other end of the line is your abundant future.

2. Consider and write down your answers to the following questions: *How do I feel about money? Do my loved ones have a good relationship with money? Are there any events in my life, my family's and ancestors' lives that might be hindering the flow of money?*

3. Once you have written down all the obvious answers, add: *All other unknown reasons are also left on the paper.*

4. Safely set the paper alight and watch it burn. This represents the final link between you and those old energies being released.

5. When you are ready, step over the line and pick up your Pyrite crystal.

Soul: To be abundant you need to make sure that the line of manifestation is flowing through all the chakras. To support this, place a Pyrite crystal specimen over the pubic bone for 20 minutes.

Additional properties: Strength, generosity, the Divine Masculine

Additional techniques: Place a natural Pyrite cube in your home when you want more strength. Keep in your wallet to attract money.

Suggested shapes: Points, nuggets, hearts, naturally formed cubes

Source: Peru, Italy, Spain

RED ARAGONITE *also called Sputnik Aragonite*

CENTRING

Made up of multiple crystal branches pointing in different directions, Red Aragonite is able to dispel negative energies away from a person or a place.

Physical: Red Aragonite can be used to redirect energies and stop any energy build-up happening in the body. Place your crystal over any area of physical discomfort for 3–5 minutes.

If you are not aware of a specific area that needs support but you still feel guided to do this process, simply place your crystal anywhere on your body and keep intuitively moving it around for as long as you feel you need to.

Emotional: If you are feeling an emotion but cannot pinpoint what it is, Red Aragonite will help you understand and process it, allowing it to be released.

Find a quiet moment and, while holding your crystal in your non-dominant hand, in your mind's eye ask the emotion why it is there and what it wants to tell you. Let any answers come: they may offer a clearer feeling of what the emotion is. Keep holding the crystal while the emotion is processed. This should only take a few moments. If it turns into a different emotion, follow the same process.

Soul: Red Aragonite can rebalance the chakras so we feel more centred. If you've chosen Red Aragonite for soul-aligned goals, this chakra balancing practice may help your goals progress more smoothly.

1. Lie down in a comfortable spot.
2. Place your crystal on your root chakra for 3 minutes. While it's there, have the intention that any build-up of energy will be dispelled.
3. Moving up the body, do the same for each chakra.
4. Once you get to the crown, start working down the body again.
5. Take the crystal away and rest for a few minutes.

Additional properties: Aura cleanse, dispels conflict, balances home environments

Additional techniques: Place under the feet to ground your energies.

Suggested shape: Raw

Source: Morocco

RED JASPER

HEALTH

Red Jasper was a favourite stone among ancient civilizations and is still a popular crystal today. Its frequency and dense red appearance indicate that it is a powerful tool for the physical world. It asks that we focus on the long term, putting in place the foundations that are needed for future success.

Interestingly, whichever of your three goals you have selected Red Jasper for, the reason will be the same. This crystal wants you to make a plan that doesn't just support you for the next few months but will offer lifelong improvements for your physical, emotional and spiritual health.

Choosing Red Jasper shows you are ready to make strategic changes for long-term improvement. It also suggests these changes may be in multiple areas of your life.

Physical: Wear Red Jasper as a ring or bracelet or put a tumble in your trouser pocket so it's positioned over the root chakra. When worn here, it can inspire us to make changes that will benefit our physical body.

Emotional: Take Red Jasper as a crystal elixir (see page 26) every other day for two weeks. During those two weeks, each morning when you wake up journal for at least 30–45 minutes. Focus on these three journal prompts, taking one each day: *What are the questions and concerns I have around my goal? How do I create stronger foundations in my life? What am I generally feeling and thinking today?* Make sure you work on each question at least twice. On the last two days I would like you to journal on *Who am I now and where am I going long term?*

Soul: Follow the journal prompts outlined above and also sleep with a large Red Jasper positioned on or over the root chakra.

Additional properties: Protection, strength, stamina, bravery

Additional techniques: Keep a Red Jasper tumble with you when you have to do something brave.

Suggested shapes: Jewellery, worry stones, symbolic shapes, tumbles

Source: India, Brazil, France, Russia, Germany, the USA

ROOT CHAKRA CRYSTALS

SMOKY QUARTZ *also called Morion Quartz*

HOPE

A museum-quality Smoky Quartz specimen includes aspects of dark brown quartz, transitioning to Clear Quartz. This represents how Smoky Quartz *leads you through the darkness into the light* or, in other words, *shows you the light at the end of the tunnel*. It offers the information, wisdom and experiences you need to see the way forwards. When you work with Smoky Quartz you need to be open to guidance coming in all forms.

Physical: To welcome in knowledge that will support your physical health, lie down and place a specimen just above the pubic bone and one on each shoulder. This triangle of crystal energy invites knowledge into your physical world for you to learn and act on.

Emotional: Smoky Quartz is the perfect crystal to work with when you have too many ideas and don't know which one to choose. Alternatively, some people work with this crystal when they don't know what their purpose is but they do know they want to be happier. This makes it the life coach of the crystal world.

When you need this kind of guidance, keep your Smoky Quartz with you at all times. It's perfect as a piece of jewellery and ideally should be worn as a ring so it sits near the root chakra. You can also keep this crystal with you at night so you can receive information in your dreams.

Soul: Choosing this crystal to support your soul-aligned goals suggests your angels and spirit guides want to connect with you to offer support. This often involves working with your psychic skills or just being attracted to a situation or event that gives you unexpected, helpful information. Keep a specimen of Smoky Quartz with you at all times, so it can show you how those communications are going to be made.

Additional properties: Grounding and protection

Additional techniques: Think of a question, then press your crystal to the third eye to activate the answer.

Suggested shapes: Jewellery, points, angels, skulls, pyramids, tumbles

Source: Worldwide

CARNELIAN

MOTIVATION

Carnelian comes in yellow, orange and red tones, connecting its energy to the bottom three chakras, the three that focus primarily on the physical world.

Physical: Carnelian welcomes in the knowledge we need to understand so we can improve our overall health. Keep a Carnelian tumble with you as much as possible, positioned over the lower three chakras. If change feels overwhelming, trust that your crystal's support will bring in moments of inspiration, intuitive thoughts or health information at the right time and in a way that you find manageable.

Emotional: Many people stifle their emotions rather than expressing them. When we do that we internalize the emotion's energy. This is another way energy around a chakra can build up. Carnelian will release any emotional build-up you might be experiencing and help you learn to process your emotions in a healthier way.

Take a few moments each week to lie down and place your crystal over your belly button then intuitively move it around your body. As you do this, hold the intention that your crystal is clearing any emotions that are there. Once you have finished, make sure you cleanse the crystal to release those energies.

In the future when new emotions come up, hold your Carnelian and have the intention that your crystal, rather than your body, will take on the emotions.

Soul: Carnelian's connection to the lower three chakras indicates it's a good crystal for goal setting. When we start a new project, its yellow tones offer us the confidence and vitality we need to get started. The orange tones support us through the project, keeping us focused. When the project is over, the red tones give us the confidence to tell others about our achievements.

This really makes Carnelian a talisman for major accomplishments. Treat yourself to a statement piece for your home or some Carnelian jewellery.

Additional properties: Creativity, fertility

Additional techniques: Crystal grids for success.

Suggested shapes: Towers, points, wands, palms, eggs, flames

Source: India, Brazil, Uruguay

COPPER

ALIGNMENT

Copper is the optimum conductor for earthing energy. That means we can deliberately use it to radiate our energy or release any excess. Other grounding tools have dense, heavy properties that pull us down so we feel connected to the ground. In contrast, Copper has a fluidity to its energy, so there is a movement to its properties. We are drawn to it when we want a connection to nature, but we also want to move and progress forwards.

Physical: Many people wear Copper jewellery to enhance their life-force energy. Copper is associated with Venus and Aphrodite, the goddesses of love. Both also represent beauty. Copper can radiate the life-force energy that enhances a person's complexion.

Emotional: Copper helps us stay focused throughout important tasks. We become attracted to Copper when we feel we are going off course and need to realign with our original goal. This is where the properties of *earthing* and *flow* work in our favour. When you feel you are losing focus, create a crystal elixir using a Copper cup or the classic elixir process outlined on page 26. Drink it once a day for at least two weeks.

Soul: Copper is an exciting selection to make because it conducts energy, suggesting you are ready to increase your vibration and heighten your spiritual connection. One way to do this is to meditate inside a Copper pyramid. Start with five-minute sessions once a week, then increase by five minutes each week until you get to 30 minutes.

If you cannot source a Copper pyramid, try using three Copper nuggets. Lie down, then place two nuggets on either side of your feet and one above your head.

Additional properties: Finding direction, grounding higher vibrations, connecting to the Earth element

Additional techniques: Place a Copper nugget under your feet to earth your energies. Use Copper to create wired jewellery so it can amplify its energies.

Suggested shapes: Nuggets

Source: Chile, Peru, China

ORANGE CALCITE

CREATIVITY

Being *in the flow* refers to the moments when inspiration comes easily to us and what we create feels magical, as if it is divinely guided. When we find our own unique form of creative expression, this experience becomes available to us all.

The bright, vivacious colours of Orange Calcite invite creativity into our lives. It asks that we explore these skills further so that divine guidance can support us.

Physical: Orange Calcite offers us the confidence to explore new ways of expressing our creativity through our physical body. For some, choosing this crystal for physical support will indicate a desire for greater sexual exploration. To achieve this, Orange Calcite is best used as a crystal elixir (see page 26).

Emotional: Orange Calcite welcomes creative thinking. It helps us think outside the box, accessing new ideas we might not have thought of before. This includes growing our emotional intelligence so we can see patterns playing out in our life and acknowledging when we are wrong. As with the physical support (see above), a crystal elixir is perfect for this kind of work.

Soul: When we are working on new projects we can feel overwhelmed. Part of the concept of *being in the flow* means throwing away the to-do list and trusting that all jobs will get done eventually, allowing us to focus on the tasks we are motivated to do, tapping into our energy body to do the jobs that match our current mood. This in turn raises our vibration, giving us the motivation to do the jobs that we have been avoiding.

Additional properties: Vitality, alignment, confidence

Additional techniques: Keep on your work desk to sustain your energies throughout the day.

Suggested shapes: Raw points, hearts, eggs, spheres

Source: Mexico

PEACH MOONSTONE

SELF-DISCOVERY

As its name suggests, this stone connects us to the Moon and its cycles, the cycles of life and female cycles. It's the perfect pregnancy and new mum crystal. Moonstone is also connected to the process of self-discovery.

Physical: This stone specifically supports the female body as it goes through adolescence, pregnancy, labour and nursing, then into menopause and post-menopause. Wear Moonstone jewellery to keep its energies close.

Emotional: Moonstone invites us to explore our sexuality and overcome any internal or external barriers to expressing our gender. Collect two Peach Moonstones. Lie down and place one on your pubic bone, the other over your heart. Put a hand on each and relax. After 10–20 minutes, try saying out loud your gender identity, sexuality or anything else you want to declare.

Soul: The subjugation of women throughout history, and that is still going on today in many places, has created what is known as *matriarchal trauma* or *the mother wound*. Selecting Peach Moonstone for soul-aligned support suggests your matriarchal line may benefit from the chance to release any past trauma you might unknowingly be holding onto.

1. Create a large circle with Peach Moonstone chips. In the centre add any photos or items that represent your ancestors.

2. Step into the circle and sit down. Imagine your ancestors (known and unknown) joining you and sitting down. Then visualize the Moonstones creating a dome of peach energy all around you.

3. Stand up and, with the intention that anything needing to be released will be released, shake the body vigorously for at least five minutes. If you need to make sounds or other movements, then do so.

4. When you are ready, sit down, see the dome disappear and your ancestors stand up and walk away.

Additional properties: Creativity, fertility, supporting the menstrual cycle

Additional techniques: On a New Moon create a crystal grid (see page 25) using Peach Moonstone for manifestation.

Suggested shapes: Points, palms, moons, hearts, symbolic carved shapes, flames

Source: Sri Lanka, India, Brazil, Madagascar, the USA, Myanmar

STILBITE

NOURISHING

Stilbite's tones, its unique appearance and the subtle caring energy it offers can be spellbinding. In a world that can be harsh and uncaring, the compassionate energies of Stilbite feel like a dramatic contrast.

Physical: Stilbite has the energy of a supporting midwife: a wise, insightful and experienced pair of hands, offering kindness and taking charge when required. This makes it the ideal crystal companion for any mother-to-be or anyone needing reassurance. Stilbite acts like a protective, supportive bubble around you. Consider placing a specimen on your bedside table so you can enjoy these energies while you sleep.

Emotional: Stilbite helps us access our clairempathy skills (the intuition that allows us to use our emotions as a form of psychic communication). Those emotions might be our own or other people's and will offer clues to specific situations we might be in.

Being attracted to this crystal suggests that you already have clairempathy, but Stilbite can help you to develop the skill further. At first, it can be hard to understand if an emotion is our own or a psychic message. Keeping a specimen of this crystal by your bed will help you learn to tell the difference.

Soul: You will often find Stilbite and Apophyllite (see page 186) together. Normally, when two crystals occur together, their properties complement each other. In this case, transparent white Apophyllite represents the spiritual world in general, while dense orange Stilbite symbolizes spirituality in the physical world. Together they help you develop a spiritual practice. This could be a morning routine such as yoga or meditation, making offerings to a shrine, praying or anything else you would consider spiritual.

Place an Apophyllite and a Stilbite crystal in the space where you plan to perform your routine in order to cultivate a strong, consistent practice.

Additional properties: Spirituality, parenting, cherishing life, harmony

Additional techniques: Keep Stilbite with you when you are cultivating a new spiritual practice.

Suggested shapes: Raw, palms

Source: India, Iceland, the UK

SUNSTONE *also called Heliolite*

EMPOWERMENT

In astrology the Sun represents how the world perceives us, as well as our willpower and sense of vitality. Sunstone works with these aspects of ourselves so we can feel confidence in how we present ourselves. It also embodies the hero archetype, the part of us that goes on quests to realize our soul purpose. Using Sunstone for this work means that any fears fall away, and we progress along our soul path with confidence, feeling comfortable in our own skin.

Physical: Sunstone is a good support for the lower back. To strengthen that area, place a stone there when you are lying down.

Emotional: Our higher self represents the ancient, highest vibrational aspect of ourselves, the one that is most closely connected to Source Energy or the Divine. Accessing this part of you calms stress and relieves negative mind chatter, replacing it with a stillness that comes from living from your highest self.

To start living more from this place of greater connection, wear a Sunstone bracelet so it's in line with your sacral chakra, enforcing those energies.

Soul: Sometimes we are presented with situations that are outside our comfort zone but that are good for our spiritual growth. In those moments, try embodying an archetype who has the characteristics you need. This could be a celebrity who has experience in the area you need support in or whose character suits the task at hand, whether it is the confidence of Beyonce, the sense of tradition of Queen Elizabeth II or the inspirational words of Dr Martin Luther King.

See that person in front of you. Put on your Sunstone jewellery and step into that space to embrace the person's energy. This represents you and your crystal taking on those characteristics. Wear your jewellery every time you want to access that energy.

Additional properties: Vitality, invoking the Fire element

Additional techniques: Hold your crystal and imagine a ray of sunshine surrounding you, cleansing and adding vitality to your body.

Suggested shapes: Points, palms, spheres, wands, jewellery, flames

Source: India, Norway, Sweden, Australia, Russia, the USA

TANGERINE QUARTZ

RESOLVE

The orange tones of Tangerine Quartz represent its connection to the sacral chakra, while its transparent aspects suggest an ability to support our energy body.

The sacral chakra is the seat of our emotions. As such it can hold the energy of past trauma, including physical and sexual trauma. Selecting Tangerine Quartz suggests that any energies that have built up in that area are ready to be released.

Physical: Support the body in releasing any trauma it might be holding by creating a crystal elixir (see page 26) with your Tangerine Quartz. Drink a full glass of elixir once a day for two weeks or until you feel a positive shift in your emotions.

Emotional: Tangerine Quartz can also help release emotional traumas from the body. To do this follow the physical steps above, but also spend some time each day putting on your favourite dance tracks and vigorously moving and shaking your body to help shift and release those old energies.

Soul: Selecting Tangerine Quartz suggests it would benefit you to feel safer and more protected. Source six small Tangerine Quartz points or tumbles plus any six black crystals: I would suggest Black Tourmaline. Place them in a large circle you can lie inside. Lie in the circle for 30 minutes once a week, so that your auric field starts to cultivate a stronger protective energy.

Additional properties: Creativity, fertility, inner child work, playfulness

Additional techniques: Keep a Tangerine Quartz point with you to welcome fun.

Suggested shapes: Raw points, clusters

Source: Brazil, Madagascar

VANADINITE

DETERMINATION

The best way to describe this crystal is that it *puts your soul into action*. More than any other crystal, Vanadinite wants you to put actions in place to make success inevitable. Its willpower and determination focus your attention on the task at hand as it wants you to see the task through to the end.

Physical: Vanadinite wants to see you moving. It likes dynamic action, so it's a perfect support for those suffering from any form of drowsiness or fatigue. For sustained energy levels, display your Vanadinite crystal near your workspace and use it to make a daily crystal elixir (see page 26). Continue taking your elixir until you have experienced several weeks of improved energy levels.

Emotional: If you are easily distracted, procrastination will stop you achieving your goal. Place a large Vanadinite specimen in your workspace and allow it to create a dome of energy around you so you stay focused.

Soul: Vanadinite has a connection to the magical energies we find in our physical surroundings. Selecting this crystal suggests you have a strong connection to *spiritual alchemy*, which means using the different energies available to us for healing work.

Mother Nature offers numerous energies we can connect to, including the astrological cycles, Moon cycles and the seasons. If you are drawn to Vanadinite, it will be suggesting these, as well as the energies of the weather, the Earth's chakra points and the ley lines, all of which might inspire your work. Meditate with Vanadinite so you can start sensing these subtle energies.

Additional properties: Stamina, discipline, psychogeography

Additional techniques: Place a specimen on top of your diary to ensure you only plan activities that are for your highest good.

Suggested shape: Raw

Source: Morocco, Mexico, Arizona

AMBER

OPTIMISM

Amber is fossilized tree resin that forms into yellow, butterscotch and brown specimens, often with insects encased inside.

Solar plexus crystals focus on aiding the organs of the abdomen, including the spleen, stomach and pancreas. When we experience worry, this can slow down the digestive process. In energy work we see this as struggling to *digest our emotions*. If we can raise our vibration above those emotions, it will help us remove those blocks and start to feel more optimistic.

Physical: To support the physical organs around the solar plexus, consider taking a glass of Amber elixir (see page 26) several days a week.

Emotional: Sadly, *I don't deserve to be happy* is a subconscious belief many of us have. Regularly wear an Amber charm on a long chain with an Amber bracelet to position as much positive energy over the solar plexus as possible.

Soul: To help heal emotions that could have past-life origins, which might explain any deep sadness, try the following:

1. Start by taking the time to journal on the question: *How is this sadness showing up in your life?* Think about what the emotions feel like, when you first experienced them and what happens when they surface.

2. Fold up the sheet of paper on which you've written your answer then cleanse it with sage in the same way you would a crystal (see page 11). By cleansing the paper you are reducing the energy of those words and the impact those emotions and events have had on your life.

3. Put the paper somewhere it can be displayed but won't be disturbed and place your Amber crystal on top of it. Leave it there for 3–4 weeks so the Amber has time to heal the energetic cords connecting you to any past-life events.

Additional properties: Helps clear depression, drive, motivation, can access other timelines

Additional techniques: Meditate with Amber in your dominant hand so you can receive images of the time the crystal was formed.

Suggested shapes: Raw, jewellery

Source: Germany, Poland, Russia

SOLAR PLEXUS CHAKRA CRYSTALS

CITRINE

MANIFESTATION

Citrine is the crystal of 'pure joy and happiness'. This is the highest frequency of emotion a human can feel. Citrine is a worldwide favourite because people resonate on a deep level with the properties it offers and the need to attract more joy into their lives. To bring these emotions into your life, it manifests experiences and things that will make you happy. Therefore Citrine is also known as a manifestation crystal.

Physical: Choosing Citrine for your physical goals suggests you aspire to be as positive as possible. Placing Citrine on the solar plexus or taking it daily as an elixir (see page 26) will motivate you to keep up with your goals.

Emotional: Sometimes we have a deep-seated belief that manifesting isn't possible. Selecting Citrine suggests we need help overcoming any limiting beliefs. Keeping Citrine near will relieve and heal those beliefs, while bringing you the lessons and knowledge you need to embrace your manifesting abilities.

Soul: Choosing Citrine as your spiritual support suggests that you are ready to raise your personal frequency and take on new, more complex spiritual lessons, to become part of a more compassionate, holistic and nature-focused global community.

The Fibonacci spiral represents manifesting energy spiralling towards you. Creating it can command the energetic spiral to begin.

1. Each morning, soon after you wake up, take a moment to place the Citrine close to your heart.
2. Close your eyes and imagine that it's several months after you have completed your current goal, and that that goal is part of your everyday life. Ask yourself how you feel now that it has been achieved.
3. Now imagine that emotion spiralling towards you.
4. Do this daily for five minutes.

Additional properties: Happiness, success, confidence

Additional techniques: When you are feeling down, wear a piece of Citrine jewellery to raise your vibration.

Suggested shapes: Points, spheres, jewellery, wands, freeform

Source: Brazil, Madagascar

GOLD

IMPOSTER SYNDROME

The majestic, noble nature of Gold puts it centre stage in all crystal therapy teachings. A symbol of the Sun, Gold is seen to represent our higher self. It asks us to show up, be seen and be proud of who we are.

Physical: This is a highly optimistic selection for a physical goal. It suggests your soul is urging you to stay focused and to strive for the best possible outcome. For physical support, try a daily Gold elixir (see page 26) or wear Gold jewellery.

Emotional: The term impostor syndrome refers to negative thoughts making us feel like a phony, believing others could do a better job. Gold asks us to embrace who we are and understand we are already perfect.

Selecting Gold suggests you are striving towards the right things but that something is holding you back. Gold has a higher vibration than yellow, so it raises your frequency above the limiting beliefs, helping you to overcome obstacles. Try to wear it on a regular basis, ideally on a long chain so that the Gold can hang over the solar plexus.

Soul: Gold is the colour of the higher solar plexus chakra. Over the solar plexus sits our Inner Sun. This is a higher vibrational aspect of our solar plexus chakra that invites us to embody our true self, free from ego and judgement. When we raise our vibration enough to be able to access this energy, it is believed our aura will shine gold. The astrological age we are currently moving into is called the Golden Age for that very reason.

To open your higher solar plexus chakra, wear Gold as much as you can. Then once a week place your Gold jewellery over the solar plexus and imagine a golden ray emanating out of it, turning your auric field gold.

Additional properties: Enables you to value yourself and connect to gods, goddesses and deities

Additional techniques: Add Gold to a ritual, altar or shrine if you want to work with a specific deity.

Suggested shape: Jewellery

Source: China, Australia, South Africa, the USA

SOLAR PLEXUS CHAKRA CRYSTALS

GOLDEN HEALER

also called Hematoid Quartz

CONFIDENCE

Golden Healer is a quartz crystal with iron inclusions, which create the golden tones. A relatively recent find, it is part of the new age of crystal discoveries that appeared in the last few decades and are here to help us transform into a more expansive, compassionate and inclusive global race. Golden Healer connects to our higher self, the part of us that has lived many lives; it reignites the wisdom and inner confidence that comes from knowing we are always OK.

Physical: Place the Golden Healer specimen on the centre of your stomach. Leave it there for a few moments, then move it around different areas of the solar plexus, as well as your back and sides.

Emotional: Golden Healer exudes the energy of the higher solar plexus (see page 104), which is associated with the colour gold. It will support any solar plexus imbalance we need to overcome and is particularly good at increasing our confidence levels.

Place some Golden Healer tumbles in a large circle. Sit in the centre and do your regular meditation or visualization practice. The circle of crystals creates a dome around you so the healing can take place. If you are also wearing some Golden Healer jewellery, the healing will continue even after the meditation.

Soul: Spiritual confidence refers to the level of confidence you have in sharing your spiritual and intuitive skills with others or talking about any metaphysical or esoteric practices you enjoy.

Try journaling on these questions: *When speaking to others, what parts of my spirituality would I rather not share? Which spiritual topics have I chosen not to share? If I could speak openly, what would I want to talk about?* Then fold up the paper and place a Golden Healer tower on top of it. This directs the intention *I would like more joy-filled spiritual conversations* to the Universe.

Additional properties: Helps with iron deficiency, multiple-life exploration, universal consciousness

Additional techniques: Take as an elixir (see page 26) to support you if you have an iron deficiency.

Suggested shapes: Spheres, towers, hearts, palms, worry stones, skulls

Source: Brazil, Madagascar

GOLDEN TIGER'S EYE

STRENGTH

Golden Tiger's Eye embodies the tiger archetype, with the energies of strength, bravery, focus and authority. These are all skills we need to achieve our goals, making this an ideal choice for growth and development.

Physical: Selecting this crystal can indicate a need for greater physical strength and stamina. Take as an indirect elixir (see page 26) to embody that energy.

Emotional: Choosing Golden Tiger's Eye may suggest there are emotional wounds or traumas that need to be healed. Golden Tiger's Eye offers the bravery you need to start that healing process.

To receive this kind of support, keep your crystal with you at all times. You can also try both the physical and the spiritual techniques given on this page, as they will add extra layers of support.

Soul: The term archetype refers to the stereotypical traits that a person or animal encapsulates. Selecting Golden Tiger's Eye suggests that embodying the personality traits of the tiger archetype will help you through future situations. This is how to do it:

1. While holding your crystal, imagine a tiger sleeping in front of you.

2. When you are ready, step forwards into its space. As you do, imagine you are embodying the tiger's characteristics. Normally the results are a heightened feeling of those energies.

3. Keep doing this as often as you need to.

Additional properties: Boosts confidence, improves productivity

Additional techniques: Place on the back to offer strength.

Suggested shapes: Tumbles, jewellery

Source: Brazil, the USA, South Africa, India, Australia

GOLDEN TOPAZ *also called Imperial Topaz*

SELF-BELIEF

Golden Topaz vibrates at the same frequency as our higher self, the part of us that has already lived many lives and knows our soul plan. When we operate from this place, this inner knowing creates a form of self-belief that comes from understanding that we cannot fail when we are doing the 'work' we are reincarnated to do.

Physical: Golden Topaz strengthens and supports all areas of the solar plexus, especially the back. Take it as an elixir (see page 26) twice a day for at least a week.

Emotional: To cultivate self-belief, start by remembering all the things you have already achieved in your life and take pride in them. Success breeds success, so while you remember these achievements create a crystal grid (see page 25) to welcome in more of that energy. Position Golden Topaz as your centre stone.

Soul: To deliberately tap into the wisdom behind this self-belief we need to connect to our gut instinct. This communicates to us via positive or negative responses to a question. Write down some yes/no questions, then hold your Golden Topaz over the solar plexus and start asking the questions. A 'yes' response will feel like a positive, contented energy in the body. In contrast a 'no' will feel like a depleting, more negative energy.

Additional properties: Divine insight, attracts support

Additional techniques: Hold your crystal in your dominant hand to enhance your clairsentience skills (see page 176).

Suggested shapes: Raw, jewellery

Source: Worldwide, but especially Brazil

SOLAR PLEXUS CHAKRA CRYSTALS

GOLD RUTILATED QUARTZ

also called Angel Hair Quartz and Venus Hair Stone

PURPOSE

Gold Rutilated Quartz is an expert manifester because it has already manifested the rutiles, the mineral compounds that grow in rod-like shapes inside the quartz crystal.

Gold Rutilated Quartz mainly comes in Clear Quartz and Smoky Quartz. Clear specimens offer clarity; they also amplify the manifesting properties of the rutiles. Smoky Quartz is perfect when there is uncertainty and you need guidance.

Physical: Sometimes we need a positive pick-me-up. Gold Rutilated Quartz can offer this. All you have to do is meditate holding your crystal in your dominant hand. If your physical goals feel overwhelming, this will increase your vitality and motivate you to focus.

Emotional: Gold Rutilated Quartz is the perfect support for all of your emotional-purpose goals. Wear the crystal on a long chain so it's close to your solar plexus. This will keep you focused on your goal.

Soul: Once a week when you are alone and can really focus on your goal, lie down and place the crystal between your heart and solar plexus. Visualize your goal and imagine you have already achieved it. Ask yourself how that feels. Then imagine a swirl of energy coming from the crystal, spiralling out and connecting to the image of your goal.

This is a Fibonacci spiral (see page 102) and is part of sacred geometry. It is symbolically manifesting energy spiralling out and bringing your goals back to you.

Additional properties: Sending luck to others, creating an uplifting space, inner child healing

Additional techniques: When you want to send positive energy to a person or place, point the rutiles towards them.

Suggested shapes: Points, freeform, double terminated points

Source: Brazil, Madagascar

 **SOLAR PLEXUS CHAKRA CRYSTALS**

HONEY CALCITE

also called Golden Calcite and Amber Calcite

SPONTANEITY

Honey Calcite asks us to *enjoy the sweetness of life*. It reminds us to take a step back and to be in the moment, to find joy in the small things and remember how blessed we already are.

Physical: Finding joy in the little things and being in the moment are good for our stress levels and overall health. This is something the Vedic teachers regularly cite. Place the Honey Calcite over your heart, allowing it to be filled with joyful energy.

Emotional: Being drawn to Honey Calcite suggests you have too much going on in your life and not enough space for spontaneity. When we don't have or find the time to check in on ourselves, this can add to feelings of stress and being overwhelmed.

If this resonates with you, it's time to mindfully schedule in some fun. Do that now. Keep the crystal on top of your diary as a reminder to safeguard those moments.

Soul: A good way to raise your vibration and manifest new things into your life is to honour all the things you already have. This is called a *gratitude practice*.

With your crystal close by, find yourself a large sheet of paper and a pen. Take at least 30 minutes to fill that whole sheet with things you are grateful for. Don't forget to include the things you might overlook, like your eyesight, the water you drink, your favourite childhood memories and moments when others have offered you support. As you write each thing down, try to acknowledge it and feel your gratitude for it.

As you work through this activity your vibration will increase, leaving you in a blissful state. From here it's easier to manifest new things into your life.

Additional properties: Motivation, joy, manifestation

Additional techniques: Use as an elixir (see page 26) to elevate your mood.

Suggested shapes: Raw, spheres, points

Source: Worldwide, but especially Mexico

LIBYAN DESERT GLASS
also called Libyan Gold Tektite

EMBODIMENT

Scientists do not understand how this crystal was formed, but they know that whatever happened was intense and dramatic. The result is a crystal with the ability to transform us rapidly. Use it to enforce your willpower, manifest and even redesign areas of your life that don't feel authentically *you*.

Libyan Desert Glass gives you access to your Akashic records: that is, the register of all past lives, lessons, skills and karma you have collected. It allows you to bring the wisdom of those lives forwards so you can embody those aspects of yourself in this lifetime. This in turn brings you the wisdom to confidently do things differently, *to live outside the box.*

Physical: The solar plexus area includes the stomach and small intestines. Just as we digest food, this area of the body also digests our emotions, helping us to process them. Selecting Libyan Desert Glass suggests the solar plexus is ready to release old emotions. To do this, place the crystal on the middle of your stomach for five minutes a day for up to two weeks.

Emotional: Selecting this magical crystal suggests it's time to embody your past-life skills. To support this transition, Libyan Desert Glass can guide you through any fears you may have of being different.

Most of us have a fundamental fear of standing out from the crowd, potentially becoming an outcast and being thrown out of the tribe, having to fend for ourselves. To realize your dreams without this sort of fear getting in the way, wear Libyan Desert Glass as often as you can. Pair it with a Black Tourmaline tumble in a coat or trouser pocket so you also feel safe and supported.

Soul: To access information from past lives, sleep with Libyan Desert Glass next to you. This allows the crystal to show you memories in your dreams or as thoughts and guidance when you are awake.

Additional properties: Promotes abstract thinking, helps us to 'digest' new ideas and concepts

Additional techniques: To bring new ideas into the body, imagine a white light coming from above, through the crown chakra, and down the spine to the solar plexus.

Suggested shapes: Raw, jewellery

Source: Libya, Egypt

MUSCOVITE MICA

COMMUNITY

Muscovite Mica is formed in sheets of sediment. The top layers create a downwards pressure on the lower ones. The pressure and heat fuse these lower layers together. However, it's still possible to peel off the thin layers one by one.

If you consider one thin sheet on its own, it's easy to rip and break. Multiple sheets together strengthen the mica, making this the crystal representation of the saying *there is strength in numbers*. In essence, it likes the support a community offers it, which translates into the energy it offers us.

Muscovite Mica is there to help us find our community. It attracts like-minded people to us, while its yellow tones give us the confidence to go out and meet new people.

Physical: Mica encourages different areas of the body to work in harmony with each other. You can place a crystal on the relevant parts of the body, but as it is very fragile you might prefer to use it as a crystal elixir instead (see page 26).

Emotional: Selecting Mica for your emotional goals suggests that being around like-minded people might be an important support for you. Take regularly as an elixir as you contemplate the idea of attracting your tribe.

Soul: Selecting Mica as your soul plan crystal indicates a major part of that plan will involve collaborations, building a community or supporting existing communities. It suggests that this is your time to go out there and help multiple people. If this feels daunting, understand that Muscovite Mica will guide you, helping you to take one step at a time so you can integrate this work with ease.

To do this I would recommend sourcing a Muscovite Mica crystal you can display in the space you use to do your soul purpose work.

Additional properties: Relieving pressure and stress, problem solving, integrating emotions

Additional techniques: When you don't understand a situation, Muscovite Mica can help you to 'join the dots'. For greater clarity, place your crystal by your bed as you sleep.

Suggested shapes: Raw, towers

Source: India, Brazil, Afghanistan

SULPHUR

DETOX

The mineral Sulphur is present in all plant, animal and human biochemistry. It protects our cells from damage. In crystal form we can embrace these properties to detox the body, mind and soul.

Physical: Ingesting too much Sulphur isn't healthy, so make sure you wash your hands after handling your crystal. However, as Sulphur is already found in our cells, using its crystals to strengthen your own natural store is always a good idea.

To do this without handling the crystal too much, I suggest displaying it high up on a shelf, for example, away from little hands and paws. Place a glass of water next to it to create an elixir (see page 26). In this way, you are benefiting from its properties without causing any harm.

Emotional: Elixirs can support our emotional wellbeing as well as our physical body, as they raise our vibration from the inside out. When you feel the onset of negative emotions, follow the steps above to make an elixir to take every day.

Soul: To revitalize your energy body, sit near your crystal and start meditating. When you feel relaxed, imagine the energy of your crystal surrounding you for 10–20 minutes. Then observe the energies going back to your crystal before you open your eyes.

Additional properties: Increases our vibrations, helps cope with sudden change and addictions

Additional techniques: Lie in a circle of Sulphur tumbles to help change old behaviour patterns.

Suggested shapes: Raw, tumbles, points

Source: Bolivia, Poland, Italy

AMAZONITE

also called Amazon Stone, Amazon Jade

BALANCE

Amazonite's turquoise tones suggest an energetic combination of heart chakra greens and throat chakra blues. It helps us learn to speak from the heart or 'speak with diplomacy'. As its name suggests, Amazonite is linked to the Amazons, a group of ancient female warriors who often surpassed their male counterparts. Although successful fighters, their exceptional diplomatic skills meant combat was not required.

Physical: Due to a lack of confidence or previous trauma, how we hold ourselves can change. We might start to collapse our posture, unconsciously limiting the space we are taking up. This can stifle the flow of energy through the chakras. To correct this, at the start of your day, take an Amazonite crystal in both hands, roll your shoulders back, engage your heart and stand confidently in mountain pose for a few minutes.

Emotional: It is time for you to stand in your power and only say yes to things that bring you joy.

Where possible, try to pre-empt any requests coming your way, so you can consider how to decline gracefully. When you want to refuse an invitation, hold your Amazonite crystal in your dominant hand and imagine the person concerned on a TV screen in front of you. See them asking their question, close your eyes, take a breath and ask your crystal how to reply. Once you have given the answer, see how the person responds. If they say anything else and you want to reply, ask the crystal what to say next.

Soul: Between the heart and throat chakra is the lesser known higher heart chakra. This offers a more expansive and compassionate heart energy. To open it up, wear an Amazonite necklace positioned directly between the heart and throat chakras.

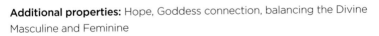

Additional properties: Hope, Goddess connection, balancing the Divine Masculine and Feminine

Additional techniques: Sit in a circle of Amazonite tumbles to strengthen your auric field.

Suggested shapes: Worry stones, palms, jewellery, tumbles

Source: Brazil, the USA, India, Madagascar, Namibia, Russia

BOTSWANA AGATE

also called Pink Banded Agate

HEALING

Composed of many layers of sedimentary rock, this crystal is a visual representation of the healing process. Choosing it indicates there has been a build-up of events and that the resulting emotions are now ready to be healed. Interestingly, our focus needs to be on the bottom, original layer of healing, which should heal those above it. The pink of the crystal reminds us to go slowly; time and love are needed to release that bottom layer.

Physical: Drink a glass of Botswana Agate elixir (see page 26) each day for a month. Before you drink, say, *I love my body and give it respect and time to heal.* You might even want to place the glass on top of the written affirmation, to program the water with it.

Emotional: Perhaps there is a specific emotion or set of emotions holding you back. The layers of the agate suggest there might be several different events, traumas or beliefs fused together, making it hard to understand where the healing should start. Write the events and emotions you can pinpoint on a piece of paper. If you think there could be other emotions as well, add *The Unknown*. Wrap this list around your crystal and place it in a spot where you go every day. Over time, move the crystal further and further away from that spot. This energetically disconnects you from those emotions so they can release and be healed.

Soul: Trauma and energetic wounds can originate in unexpected places, and selecting Botswana Agate suggests the cause of the issue could be in one of these places. Source both a Botswana Agate tumble and an Elestial Quartz crystal (see page 190), then follow the steps for emotional support given above, but this time binding both crystals and the note together.

Additional properties: Helping with grief, revealing what is hidden, heart health

Additional techniques: Create a triangle-shaped crystal grid (see page 25) with Pink Botswana Agate to unearth the truth.

Suggested shape: Tumbles

Source: Botswana

EMERALD *also called Green Beryl*

WISDOM

This semi-precious stone has one of the highest vibrations of green light in the crystal world, which is why it is one of the most impactful and healing of the heart chakra crystals. Green represents growth and learning, so selecting Emerald to support your goals suggests there are lessons to learn in order to produce a successful outcome. Emerald also supports us through heartache and break-ups, helping us learn from what has happened and understand how to avoid the same thing happening in the future.

Physical: Choosing an Emerald indicates that all areas of the body that are part of the heart chakra area would benefit from being bathed in the high frequency of Emerald's green ray. Consider sourcing an Emerald necklace that you can wear regularly. It would also be beneficial to attend a regular crystal bowl sound bath. When played, crystal bowls offer a specific frequency that clears energy build-up from the body. Wear your Emerald necklace so that the sound frequencies can help remove the energies your crystal is helping you release.

Emotional: Journal with your Emerald crystal to understand why you are repeating the same negative patterns in life. Write a question you would like answering, then place your crystal in your dominant hand. Ask the crystal your question and see what answers come.

Soul: To support the growth of your spiritual body and to progress your spiritual goals, try imagining the energy of your crystal all around you. This invites the energies closer so they can work faster.

While meditating, imagine your Emerald crystal in front of you. See it expanding until it's large enough for a door to appear on one side. Visualize yourself opening that door and going into your crystal. Once you are inside, imagine yourself sitting down so you can carry on meditating. Stay there for at least five minutes. Then watch yourself stand up and leave the crystal. See the crystal return to its original size and then open your eyes.

Additional properties: Divine wisdom, karmic patterns, learning life's lessons

Additional techniques: Hold over the heart to develop your clairsentience skills (see page 176).

Suggested shapes: Jewellery, tumbles

Source: Brazil, Egypt, Colombia

FLOWER AGATE

also called Cherry Blossom Agate

GROWTH

This crystal's alternative name, Cherry Blossom Agate, encapsulates its main property: *helping you blossom into your best self.*

Manifestation energies run through our chakras, supporting us as we work on our goals. At the point when the energies enter the heart, we either fall in love with a project, or motivation fizzles out. This acts as a gauge, motivating us to progress only the projects that are for our highest good. The problem is that our stressful lives and the disconnect with our energy body may mean we miss these signs. Flower Agate awakens greater awareness in us.

Physical: Flower Agate is a good support when placed against the back of the heart, which represents our past. Source some crystal chips you can sprinkle on the floor and lie on top of them while they do their work. This agate is so energetically gentle you could even sleep in this position. Alternatively, sprinkle your crystals on a patch of grass: this will give a deeper connection to nature and also act as a cushion as you lie on them.

Emotional: You may be lacking the passion and motivation you need in order to achieve and grow. To help, invigorate the energies around the heart chakra with a crystal elixir (see page 26), as the heart is connected to the Water element, which in turn supports the emotional body.

Soul: Perhaps you have a latent ability to gain intuitive information through the heart, which is now ready to be reawakened. When we expand our heart chakra energy, we can pick up intuitive messages. Try creating a large circle of Flower Agate chips or tumbles and sitting in the centre. Close your eyes, relax, then imagine a ring of pink light around you. As you breathe out, let that ring increase until it is in line with the crystal ring. Practise asking your heart a question, then in your mind's eye, see which reply comes.

Additional properties: Grounding, self-development

Additional techniques: Display in a calming space in order to feel more connected to nature.

Suggested shapes: Chips, tumbles, palms, flames, towers

Source: Madagascar

GREEN AVENTURINE

RECONNECTION

Healing work relating to the heart can feel heavy and very serious. In contrast, Green Aventurine is one of the most effective heart chakra crystals and it works with lightness and ease. It uses the energy of light-hearted humour to move those old memories and emotions, knowing that joy and laughter can make all the difference.

Physical: Green Aventurine is all about replenishing and regrowth. It also supports the physical heart, its surrounding organs and the circulatory system. To allow its healing vibration to go deep into the cells, try a crystal elixir (see page 26). Start by taking it once a day for two weeks, then drink it when you intuitively feel called to do so.

Emotional: Do you feel you might be stifling emotions so you don't have to feel them? It is important to release emotions in the moment they are happening, so we can keep our energies flowing freely. When this is not possible, crystals like Green Aventurine can help transmute them.

Simply carry it in a top pocket (or your bra) or place a crystal over the heart while you sleep so the energies can release slowly. You may not feel them leaving, but if a wave of emotion does arise, honour it by giving it a moment to be there. It will soon move on.

Soul: When we are drawn to Green Aventurine for soul-aligned work, it could be that the heart chakra would like a rebalance. This is important as we always want a clean flow of energy running through all the chakras. To balance this chakra, carry out the chakra balance outlined on page 18. Use your Green Aventurine crystal over the heart chakra, with a Clear Quartz next to it to amplify the energies.

Additional properties: Growth, luck, good fortune

Additional techniques: Position a Green Aventurine point so it's facing you to send good fortune in your direction.

Suggested shapes: Hearts, tumbles, points

Source: Brazil, China

GREEN JADE *also called Nephrite, Jadeite*

LUCK

We are often drawn towards symbols of good luck when the obvious routes are not working for us. Jade won't just inject more hope into our lives, it will also raise our vibration so we can experience more 'luck' as well. Lucky people are experts at manifesting. They instinctively think about what they want, send that energy out into the world and, like a magnet, it comes towards them.

These people don't have limiting beliefs stopping 'lucky experiences' coming to them. For example, if you are dreaming of something that deep down you don't feel worthy of receiving, you manifest not receiving it. We are all good at manifesting, but some of us manifest things we do not want.

Physical: Jade is good for strengthening all areas of the physical body connected to the heart chakra, including the arms and hands. For this kind of support, sleep with a specimen between the shoulder blades (allowing for a close connection to the heart). After that, sleep with your crystal placed anywhere you feel it needs to be positioned.

Emotional: Selecting Green Jade to support your emotional goals suggests there are limiting beliefs to heal so that luck *can* work for you. Wear Jade as often as you can.

Ideally, place it over the heart to heal any beliefs held there. At the same time, program a Clear Quartz crystal to heal any limiting beliefs you have (see page 188). That way anything holding you back can also be healed.

Soul: Selecting Green Jade as your spiritual support suggests the reasons you need more luck in your life are coming from a previous lifetime. To overcome this, wear Green Jade earrings. We have a chakra behind each ear connected to our past lives, so this alignment will support its healing.

Additional properties: Supports the urinary system, heals our relationships with money, encourages growth

Additional techniques: Place over the kidneys to release fear from the body.

Suggested shapes: Palms, jewellery

Source: Japan, Myanmar, Guatemala, Russia, Canada, New Zealand, China

MALACHITE

PAIN

Malachite is the crystal for emotional and physical pain. It acts as a sponge, drawing the excess energy build-up from the body and storing it in the crystal until it can be cleansed.

Physical: To relieve physical pain in the body, place your Malachite crystal over that area. Leave it there as long as you can. Twenty minutes is a good length of time.

Emotional: To release emotions trapped in the body using Malachite, close your eyes and calm your breath. With the crystal over your heart ask: *Where in my body is the emotion trapped?* If an answer comes, ask your crystal what the emotion is and why it is there. Then move your crystal to that location. Relax and leave it in place for up to 20 minutes. If it falls off before then, that is a sign it's done.

Soul: Our energy body can also suffer wounds from previous lives. This can affect our current life, through unexplained deep sadness, a lack of drive or fears and limiting beliefs. About 1m (3ft) above our head is our soul star chakra. This is normally a magenta colour and is the home of our soul energy, also called our higher self. To heal ourselves at this deeper level we need to send the Malachite energy to our soul star. Start by sitting down, holding your Malachite in your dominant hand, and close your eyes and relax. Imagine a green energy coming out of the crystal and surrounding your body. Then imagine your soul star, a ball of pearlescent magenta light about 1m (3ft) above you. Send the green energy to your soul star and see it surrounding the sphere. Stay like this for roughly 5–10 minutes, then see the energy leave your soul star and go back to the crystal.

Additional properties: Soul purpose

Additional techniques: Create a circle of tumbles around the body to heal any energetic wounds in the auric field.

Suggested shapes: Slabs, tumbles, raw

Source: Congo, Russia, the USA, Morocco, Namibia

MOLDAVITE

SELF-ACCEPTANCE

Moldavite is a tektite formed when an asteroid hit the Moldova River in Bohemia, now part of the Czech Republic. Its main property is 'offering us alien concepts'. This is inspired by the idea that the asteroid has travelled through space from unknown, unseen locations, so it has the potential to offer knowledge and wisdom we haven't experienced before.

Physical: Moldavite will offer powerful healing for the physical body. Place between the heart and throat for five minutes a day, every day for a week. In week two, increase that by a minute each day, until you get to 10 minutes.

Note that this is a high-vibrational crystal that can feel buzzy even for people who normally can't feel crystal energy. As you become familiar with its energy, I'd recommend having it with you for a maximum of only 20 minutes each day.

Emotional: Do you feel different to other people? Is there a disconnect between who you are and what your heart wants? When we feel like this, often our path to happiness is less ordinary. This is when Moldavite can bring in its *alien concepts* to help us understand and see things differently, so that we can find our own unique form of happiness.

Soul: Many people feel that being in nature offers them a connection to something greater. Others experience that divine connection when looking at the galaxies. To feel that connection we need our stellar gateway chakra to be open. On page 134 I speak about the soul star chakra opening. This is about 1m (3ft) above us and connects us to our higher self. Above that is our stellar gateway chakra, which is our connection to the galaxies. To strengthen that connection, sit in meditation and imagine a white light travelling up through your body to your crown chakra, then up to the soul star. Let it stay there for a moment. Then keep travelling up to the stellar gateway, which is a large pearlescent ball of golden light. From there visualize the light travelling down again, moving through the body and into the ground.

Additional properties: Combats fungal infections and parasites, accelerates spiritual healing, lucid dreaming

Additional techniques: Wear at night to stimulate astral travel.

Suggested shapes: Raw, jewellery

Source: Czech Republic

MORGANITE

also called Pink Beryl, Rose Beryl, Pink Emerald

GRIEF SUPPORT

Morganite is a compassionate Water element crystal that supports us through the grieving process. It energetically creates space for us and offers support and protection while we process our loss.

You might have selected Morganite if you are grieving for a loved one, but we can experience grief for the loss of anything we love dearly. Consider the sadness felt when someone loses a job they enjoy, doesn't achieve the grades they need for the course they want to progress to or loses touch with a beloved friend. In that moment, these are also losses to be grieved.

Physical: Ageing, experiencing menopause or losing our good health are also losses that may need to be grieved. Selecting Morganite for your physical body suggests that its compassionate energies will support the body through this process. Simply go to sleep with your crystal specimen placed over the relevant area.

Emotional: Being a Water element crystal, Morganite is good at helping us process and work through the most complex of emotions. In times of grief, wearing Morganite will help you understand how important it is to give yourself the time and space you need. It will create a protective bubble of support around you.

Soul: Morganite has a heavenly energy that can help us feel closer to those who have passed. For this reason I would recommend displaying a Morganite specimen by your bedside.

Additional properties: Relieves loneliness, calms the ego, supports relationships

Additional techniques: Gift Morganite to a friend to show how important they are to you.

Suggested shapes: Raw, tumbles, jewellery

Source: Brazil, Madagascar, Afghanistan, China

MOSS AGATE

CONNECTS TO NATURE

Moss Agate appears to have plants and foliage hiding inside it, making it the perfect representation of the natural world.

Physical: If your physical body is being drawn to Moss Agate, it probably wants to spend more time out in nature. If you are in a location that restricts frequent access to the natural world, you can place crystals around your body to recreate this experience.

Simply lie down and position your favourite Moss Agate over your heart. Close your eyes and take some deep breaths. Spend a moment connecting to your crystal, moving it around in your hands. Now imagine you are lying in a meadow, a forest of trees in the distance, wildflowers moving in the breeze and birds in the sky. Allow yourself to fully enjoy the moment before you remove your crystal and open your eyes.

Emotional: Ayurveda, which is another aspect of the Vedic teachings, suggests that a connection to nature is something to prioritize, as it benefits all aspects of our body, mind and soul. Consider how often you intentionally go out into nature. Selecting Moss Agate suggests increasing the amount of time spent in nature would be the perfect support for your current goal. Gift yourself a Moss Agate crystal and display it prominently in your home to bring nature's energies into your space.

Soul: This book focuses on the main seven chakras, but we know there are more. One is called the Earth star chakra – positioned 1m (3ft) beneath us, it helps cultivate an appreciation for the natural world. If you are drawn to crystals, you already have an open Earth star chakra. To support it, lie down and place a Moss Agate crystal about 1m (3ft) below your feet for 10 minutes. This will energize and regulate this chakra.

Additional properties: Promotes growth, calms animals

Additional techniques: Display by your houseplants to help them grow.

Suggested shapes: Leaves, hearts, tumbles, palms

Source: India, Brazil, Uruguay

PERIDOT *also called Olivine*

POSITIVITY

Peridot is a quick injection of positivity. Choosing it is a sign that actively lifting your energies will offer you a positive energetic shift. Its olive tone was originally connected with the Divine Feminine. A mix of yellow and green, together these colours create a bridge between the solar plexus and heart chakras, linking the most joyful energies of the solar plexus with the compassionate, healing energies of the heart.

Physical: Positive energy is a catalyst for healing the physical body. Take Peridot as a daily elixir (see page 26), but also wear it as jewellery – ideally a necklace with a long chain so the crystal can sit between the heart and the solar plexus chakras.

Emotional: Selecting Peridot for emotional support suggests there may be long-standing and perhaps quite deep-seated painful or depressive emotions that are ready to be seen and healed.

Peridot wants us to understand the saying *Where our attention goes, energy flows*. This is the essence of the *law of attraction*, a universal law highlighting the fact that what we notice, we will see more of. Therefore, when we are low we need to actively look for positive things to lift our energies. This might be hard to comprehend right now, but follow the steps given for physical guidance above, while also actively looking for things in your everyday life that bring you joy.

Soul: Sometimes a residual sadness can linger from a past life. Peridot is good at helping lift this old energy. Lie down and place the crystal about 1m (3ft) above you, so it is positioned over your soul star. Stay there for up to 30 minutes. Then replace your Peridot with a Black Tourmaline under your feet to ground yourself before you stand up.

Additional properties: Divine Feminine, raises vibrations

Additional techniques: Place Peridot chips in a circle around your body to fill the auric field with positivity.

Suggested shapes: Chips, jewellery, raw

Source: Australia, Pakistan, China, Egypt, Sri Lanka

ROSE QUARTZ *also called Pink Quartz*

SELF-LOVE

Rose Quartz combines the two most prominent properties of the pink heart chakra crystals: romantic love and self-love. Most people are drawn to this crystal at some point, as those properties are the two fundamental needs we all look to achieve in life.

Physical: All areas of our body that are connected to the heart chakra benefit from the vibration of love. The more we can surround ourselves in this energy, the happier our bodies will be. A crystal elixir is a good way to do this, but you can also try a crystal elixir bath. You make this the same way you would make a crystal elixir (see page 26), but place the crystal in or near the bathwater so that the water picks up the crystal's vibrations. Consider also lighting rose-scented candles and adding rose petals to the bath.

Emotional: We all deserve to enjoy self-love, but events in our past might need healing before we can truly 'love ourselves'. Find a space in your home where you can go each day for 21 days and journal on the questions: *Why do I deserve self-love? What is stopping me achieving self-love?* In that space, create a crystal grid (see page 25) to bring in the energies of self-love. Use a Rose Quartz specimen as your centre stone and Botswana Agate as your desire stones. Each day, sit next to your crystal grid as you journal. Some days the same answers may come, on other days new layers of information may arise that need to be healed.

Soul: Our heart chakra is the gateway between the lower and upper chakras. The lower chakras need to be fully open before we can access the higher ones. Once they are all open, we need to cultivate a steady flow of energy between them all. To do this, follow the chakra balance on page 18 while tracing the line of the chakras up and down the body using a Rose Quartz wand.

Additional properties: Helps with self-forgiveness, strengthens relationships, encourages romance

Additional techniques: Keep a heart-shaped crystal with you when you want to invite a new romantic relationship into your life.

Suggested shapes: Hearts, palms

Source: Madagascar, Brazil, China

WATERMELON TOURMALINE

also called Bi-coloured Tourmaline

FORGIVENESS

When something happens that requires forgiveness, thoughts can play over in our minds, emotions are naturally high and the surrounding energy can feel dense and overpowering. It's important to process emotions as much as possible so they don't build up, but if it feels too soon to consider forgiveness, start 'releasing' the energy around it with the intention that one day you will be ready.

If we can try to understand the lessons a situation offers us, being ready to forgive can happen sooner. The Green Tourmaline aspect of Watermelon Tourmaline helps us reach that place, while the Pink Tourmaline holds us in a bubble of love, supporting us through the process and offering hope.

Physical: Your body may want to release any energy that is building up. Source a necklace with a long chain and wear it down your back so the crystal sits over the back of your heart. This allows it to soothe the back heart chakra which has a focus on past events.

Emotional: A daily Watermelon Tourmaline crystal elixir (see page 26) is a powerful support during an emotive time. Follow the physical technique above to help support the healing.

Soul: You may be being guided to do the big work and allow yourself to forgive. Revered by ancient Central and South American civilizations, cacao opens and expands our heart energies so we can heal. Each morning for 21 days, put on your Watermelon Tourmaline necklace, then create a cacao drink (8–10g/about $^1/_3$ oz of cacao is perfect for micro-dosing). Sitting in silence, slowly sip your drink. As you do, imagine the pink and green energies of your crystal surrounding you. Take a moment after each sip to contemplate where the energies of the drink go in the body.

Additional properties: Soothes grief, trauma release, calms PTSD, helps children process traumatic events

Additional techniques: Wear daily to support the processing of trauma.

Suggested shapes: Raw, jewellery

Source: Africa, Brazil, the USA

ANGELITE *also called Anhydrite*

ANGELIC COMMUNICATION

Blue throat chakra crystals support all forms of communication, including communication with angels and our guardian angel, but Angelite offers more practical real-world support. This is reflected by its dense physical appearance.

Physical: To offer the physical body angelic healing, place a small Angelite tumble on the throat or use the crystals to create an elixir (see page 26).

Emotional: Selecting Angelite as your blue crystal suggests that cultivating a relationship with your guardian angel would offer you reassuring support. Sometimes we can struggle to connect to our angels, due to latent beliefs around their existence or not feeling deserving of their time. To overcome this, find an angel-shaped Angelite and display it in a room you sit in every day. Over time, move it closer to your seat so you can become increasingly familiar with its energy, while also energetically overcoming any blocks that stop you connecting to your angels. You might start to see repeating patterns, synchronicities, images of angels or the same symbol appearing regularly. This is commonly how angels choose to communicate with us.

Soul: Angelic communication often plays out via clairaudient skills (the ability to hear psychic messages), particularly in the moments before we fall asleep or just after we wake up. Selecting Angelite for spiritual support suggests firstly that this skill is available to you and secondly that your angels want to start working with you to help you achieve your goals. To open up to clairaudient messages, position the crystal close to your ears, either by wearing Angelite earrings or by sleeping with Angelite under your pillow.

Additional properties: Comforts young children and pets, creates a safe space, connects to the Air element

Additional techniques: Display by the bedside to help you sleep.

Suggested shapes: Angels, worry stones, jewellery, tumbles, hearts

Source: Peru

AQUAMARINE

SELF-EXPRESSION

Known as 'Water of the Sea', Aquamarine exudes Water element energies. Poseidon, god of the sea and water, is closely connected to Aquamarine. Through him, mermaids and the ancient lost civilization of Atlantis are also associated with this crystal.

All of these connections to the Water element translate as a powerful emotional support crystal. Aquamarine helps overcome anything that is stopping you from speaking your divine truth. Imagine it washing away those fears so that you can make changes.

Physical: With such a strong connection to the Water element, Aquamarine is perfect as a crystal elixir (see page 26). To support the throat chakra area, take it every day for at least a week.

Emotional: Aquamarine wants us to communicate from our highest truth. From there your energy is pure, allowing you to feel a greater confidence in your own unique form of self-expression. Wearing an Aquamarine necklace or earrings naturally helps cultivate this skill.

Soul: Clearing our energy field is something we should do on a regular basis, as old, unprocessed emotions can build up as energies stored in the body. We might be drawn to Aquamarine when there is a memory of past-life wounds still being held in our energetic field.

We can use this crystal to draw on the energy of water for this kind of healing. Start by taking a shower while you hold the intention that you are washing away anything that is there. Once you are out of the shower, wear blue clothing so you are wrapping your body in that energy. Finish by moving your Aquamarine crystal around your body in a brushing motion to remove any remaining unwanted energy.

Additional properties: Connects you to the oceans and different water sources around the world

Additional techniques: Aquamarine can be worn as a talisman to promote safety when travelling.

Suggested shapes: Jewellery, raw

Source: Pakistan, Brazil, Africa, Russia

BLUE CHALCEDONY

CALMING

You could gaze into the captivating tones of Blue Chalcedony for hours. Just looking at it calms the mind and nervous system. It is hypnotic.

Physical: If you are nervous about an approaching event or generally want to support your nervous system, consider drinking a Blue Chalcedony elixir (see page 26) on a regular basis. Take the elixir once a week, then daily as you build up to the big day. You might also want to take your crystal with you to the event.

Emotional: Is there a person or situation in your life that causes you great stress and anxiety? If the answer is yes, and you feel safe in doing so, imagine meeting with that person or being in that situation. Consider what it feels like and the emotions that arise. Now imagine placing a Blue Chalcedony crystal between you and those feelings. Has it made things easier? If not, keep moving the crystal around, perhaps also making it bigger or smaller, until you start feeling better.

In the future when those situations arise, close your eyes and imagine energetically placing the crystal in that spot beforehand so that its energy is already there to support you.

Soul: Looking deep into the sphere of Blue Chalcedony, there is a depth which resembles a void, an empty space ready to be filled by anything. A Blue Chalcedony sphere is perfect for scrying work. This is the act of quietly observing something up close, in order to focus the mind and welcome in psychic or intuitive guidance. Start by bringing your Blue Chalcedony sphere up to your eyeline, then, while you lengthen your breath, look deep into the crystal. Allow a few minutes to pass, then look for signs in the shapes that the light makes on the crystal or allow intuitive ideas and sensations to come.

Additional properties: Supports the ears and mouth, cultivates peace

Additional techniques: If you feel burned out, wear Blue Chalcedony to support the nervous system.

Suggested shapes: Raw, jewellery, spheres

Source: Worldwide

BLUE KYANITE

INTUITIVE COMMUNICATION

Derived from the Greek word *kyanos*, meaning 'deep blue', Blue Kyanite embraces these calming tones to help lead us into a meditative state. From there it is much easier to connect to our intuition.

Many people associate purple third eye crystals with intuitive work, as they help us receive messages. However, once we have a message, we need blue throat chakra energies to translate it into something we can understand and communicate to others. Blue Kyanite is perfect for cultivating this skill.

Physical: To offer the body physical support, place your crystal horizontally on the throat. Keep it there for 3–5 minutes, then intuitively move it to another throat chakra area (see pages 32–3).

Emotional: It may be time to listen to your intuition for guidance. To support you, Blue Kyanite can alleviate any fears about receiving intuitive or psychic messages. Your intuition can be your greatest teacher and the best form of guidance available to you. Select a Blue Kyanite as a talisman, indicating to the Universe that you are ready to open up your intuitive skills. You might even want to wear it as a necklace so the energies are near the throat chakra.

Soul: Sometimes people receive intuitive messages that are hard to decipher. When this is happening, the flow of energy between the third eye and throat chakra needs to be strengthened so that we can translate and then communicate the message. To define this line, lie down and place your Blue Kyanite along the length of your nose or across your lips. This is the space between the third eye and the throat chakra. Placing a crystal here for three minutes twice a week recreates a connection between the two so that intuitive communication becomes possible.

Additional properties: Light language activation, channelled guidance, directs calming energies, clears meridian lines

Additional techniques: Wear over the throat to encourage clairaudient skills.

Suggested shapes: Jewellery, raw, towers

Source: Brazil, Australia, Zimbabwe

BLUE LACE AGATE

SHYNESS

Blue Lace Agate is a worldwide favourite. Its properties resonate with most people, and it works by subtly releasing energy around the throat. Light healing energies such as this are best for the throat chakra. A lot of our most complicated emotions come from moments of difficult communication, so it makes sense that this chakra can have the most layers of emotions to work through. These layers are represented by the lines in these crystals and, although they are the lines of sediment in the rock, within crystal healing they represent *working through the layers of an issue.*

Physical: To support any areas of the throat chakra, place a small crystal chip there, leaving it there for 3–5 minutes maximum. If it falls off, the work is done. Alternatively, you can follow the crystal elixir steps below.

Emotional: To achieve your emotional purpose goal, selecting Blue Lace Agate suggests there are wounds to be healed that relate to old conflicts. Alternatively, there might be a level of shyness that is holding you back. For either of these, a Blue Lace Agate elixir (see page 26) is the perfect tool. Take it daily for two months. In the first week take one sip each day, then increase the number of sips each week until you are drinking the full glass.

Soul: When we are looking for more clarity around our goals, we can work with the complementary colour of the crystal we are drawn to. In this case it is yellow. Go to the yellow crystal selection on page 51 and choose the crystal you are drawn to. Then display it next to your Blue Lace Agate. This will invite in information around any lesson you need to learn so you can work on your goal successfully.

Additional properties: Supports the body's respiratory system, soothes, cultivates acceptance

Additional techniques: Hold in your dominant hand to calm anger.

Suggested shapes: Jewellery, chips, tumbles

Source: South Africa

THROAT CHAKRA CRYSTALS

BLUE TOPAZ

ASSERTIVENESS

Collectively the members of the topaz family have a high Mohs hardness (the scale on which a crystal's hardness is measured). This means they are stronger than most crystals, which correlates to an assertive energy, protecting you and giving you the ability to stand your ground when you know you are right.

This is particularly useful when others are trying to present you in a bad light or are involving you in their lies. Blue Topaz helps you to operate from your higher self, enabling you to speak out and stand up for yourself.

Physical: If you feel as if you have the weight of the world on your shoulders, place your Blue Topaz crystal on each shoulder for five minutes and imagine those energetic weights lifting and travelling into the crystal. When you have finished, cleanse your crystal to release that energy.

Emotional: When emotions are high and are preventing reconciliation, wear this crystal so that it's easier for you to speak your divine truth. Blue Topaz will help you be more assertive, while also helping you look for a balanced outcome that is good for all concerned, rather than trying to win the argument.

Soul: Sometimes we would like to have a conversation to help heal a situation, but it may seem impossible: perhaps the person involved has passed or moved away, you simply can't reconcile or it is unsafe to meet them. In those circumstances, try having the conversation intuitively. Follow the intuitive writing steps on page 168, but hold your Blue Topaz crystal and direct your questions at the other person. If possible, share exactly how you feel and what you need from the situation. Then write their reply, and allow them to say how they feel about your joint circumstances.

Additional properties: Light language activation, channelled guidance, directs calming energies, clears meridian lines

Additional techniques: Wear over the throat to encourage clairaudient skills.

Suggested shapes: Jewellery, raw, towers

Source: Brazil, Australia, Zimbabwe

CHRYSOCOLLA

COMMUNICATION WOUNDS

Chrysocolla has long been connected to the Divine Feminine. Its blue tones speak of its ability to support communication, while the green energies of the heart chakra support safe expression. Historically this kind of energy guided the wise women to express their opinions, using words that would be received as wisdom. In cultures where the female voice is still suppressed, Chrysocolla is available to us to heal those ancestral wounds and help society welcome more diverse opinions.

Many people, myself included, see Malachite (page 134) as the sister stone of Chrysocolla. Malachite helps to heal our emotional and physical pain. Use these two crystals in tandem to work through communication wounds.

Physical: Place one small Chrysocolla specimen on your throat, one on your heart and one on each shoulder. Stay there for 20 minutes.

Emotional: Communication is the source of many of our emotional wounds. Make a list of all the things you regret saying to others or wish that you had said, then a separate list of things that have been said to you over the years that have upset you. Now pinpoint an incident which, if healed, would make the most positive impact in your life. Hold your Chrysocolla crystal in one hand and ideally a Malachite crystal in the other. Close your eyes and visualize that person (if you feel safe seeing them), and tell them *how that situation made you feel, how you wish it had played out and what you need from them now.* Give them a chance to reply. Keep going until the situation is resolved.

Soul: In order to move forwards, it is time to honour the matriarchal line you have come from, acknowledging that their potential silence has now allowed you a voice. Source a small Chrysocolla crystal and, while holding it in your non-dominant hand, contemplate what life might have been like for them. Send them gratitude and then go outside and find a particularly beautiful spot to bury your crystal as an offering of gratitude to them.

Additional properties: Alleviates stress-related symptoms, soothes tension and trauma

Additional techniques: To support the healing process, hold a tumble or worry stone while taking part in holistic therapies or counselling.

Suggested shapes: Raw, jewellery, worry stones, palms, hearts

Source: The USA, Africa

LABRADORITE *also called Spectrolite*

PSYCHIC COMMUNICATION

Labradorite helps us identify our psychic abilities, so you will only be drawn to it when you are ready to develop these skills. From a distance this crystal can look like a normal rock, but as you get closer you can see its colourful flashes running over the surface. These flashes come in all aspects of the colour spectrum, but for psychic communication we will focus on blue, which is the most common colour flash.

Physical: To support the area of the throat chakra, source 5–10 blue flash Labradorite chips. Lying down, place them intuitively from your collarbone up to your jaw. You might even want to place some behind your shoulder blades, neck and the lower part of your head. Stay there for 3–5 minutes.

Emotional: If you are drawn to Labradorite, psychic and intuitive skills are available to you, but inherited fears are stopping them from being fully developed. To aid in releasing these old energies or any more obvious fears, place a pinch of sage, mugwort or hibiscus petals in a bowl with some Labradorite crystal chips. This allows the crystal's energy to infuse with the herbs. The next day, remove the crystals. Then pick up a charcoal tablet with a pair of tongs, light it and place it in a pan, or something else in which you can safely burn the blessing. With the intention of releasing old wounds, place the herbs over the charcoal and see them start to smoke. The rising smoke symbolizes old belief systems and energetic wounds leaving you.

Soul: You may be ready to fully embody your intuitive skills. Try displaying a Labradorite specimen on your bedside table to open up those abilities, as the subconscious mind is more susceptible while you sleep.

Additional properties: Activates the Earth star chakra (see page 140), strengthens our auric field, protects us against psychic attack

Additional techniques: If you are cultivating a relationship with a deity, god or goddess, display a Labradorite carving of them on your altar or ritual space to welcome in their guidance.

Suggested shapes: Carved shapes, talisman shapes, jewellery

Source: Madagascar, Canada, Finland, China, the USA

LARIMAR *also called Blue Pectolite*

ANXIETY

The blue tones of Larimar look like rippling waves, and many people describe feeling a wave of energy wash over them as they hold this crystal. All blue crystals help calm the body but, with its added connection to the Water element, Larimar is an expert at this.

Physical: When you know you are going into a stressful situation, keep your Larimar crystal with you. This will help calm and regulate the nervous system. If you don't have your crystal with you, as soon as you can be alone, place a Black Tourmaline under your feet to ground your energies and lie down holding your Larimar crystal in your dominant hand.

Emotional: Larimar can also help relieve long-term anxiety. To do this, hold your crystal in your dominant hand and close your eyes. Visualize a beautiful waterfall in front of you. Then, with the intention that you want to release your anxieties, see yourself confidently walk under the water, allowing it to carry the energies away. Once they have gone, see yourself step away from the waterfall, then open your eyes.

Soul: Larimar has a deep connection to ancient civilizations and can access old energies to heal past-life wounds. Take some time to relax your breath and calm the body. Then start the following visualization.

Take a walk through a magical forest where everything is brighter and more colourful. After a while you find yourself approaching a crystal temple made of Larimar. You go inside and lie down on a healing bed. Imagine the crystal energy all around you. Stay there enjoying this healing for as long as you can. When you are ready, see yourself stand up, leave the temple and go back through the forest.

Additional properties: Relieves anxiety, connects to the mythical island of Atlantis and to whales and dolphins

Additional techniques: Use in an elixir (see page 26) to soothe anxieties and the symptoms they can cause.

Suggested shapes: Raw, jewellery, water droplets, mini spheres, tumbles

Source: Dominican Republic

SODALITE

TRUTH

Sodalite helps us cultivate intuitive 'knowings' so we can see the truth when it isn't obvious. When we question what others might be saying to us and when we need to be 'true to ourselves', this is especially relevant. We already use positive and negative energies to help us consider options – we get a buzz of positive energy when we're excited about a task, or unease when it's something we don't want to do. That positive or negative reaction is part of our fight or flight response, which offers an instinctive reaction to good or bad ideas. Sodalite embraces these natural physical responses and uses them to signal to us a truth or a lie.

Physical: It's hard to go through life without telling or receiving a few untruths. When we tell lies, our bodies energetically do not like it. This can result in a build-up of energy around the throat chakra. To release it, place a Sodalite chip on the throat and leave it there for 3–5 minutes. Do this bi-weekly for up to six weeks.

Emotional: If you find it hard to trust others, Sodalite can help heal any underlying reasons for distrust. It will also heighten your discernment to receive clear guidance you can rely on in the future. Three times a week for four weeks, create an indirect crystal elixir (see page 26). Each day increase the sips you take so that by the last week you are drinking the full glass.

Soul: If the truth or the right way forwards isn't clear, try working with a pyramid-shaped crystal. It represents two sides of an argument with the truth in the centre. Use it to create a crystal grid that enhances your natural instincts. The pyramid would be the centre stone. For further instructions see page 25.

Additional properties: Clarifies relationship patterns, cultivates personal values

Additional techniques: When you feel you have not handled a situation well, sleep with a Sodalite crystal next to your bed to have clarity about how you would do it differently in the future.

Suggested shapes: Pyramids, spheres, chips, tumbles

Source: Brazil, Canada, Bolivia, Myanmar

TANZANITE

DIPLOMACY

Taking time to think about your words before you utter them will make those words more impactful. Tanzanite teaches you to take time to connect to your higher self and consider the energies of the people you are talking to so that you can be sure your words are received well.

Tanzanite also teaches us what aligned communication is. It brings together the three aspects of diplomatic communication: clear expression, empathy and intuition. When this happens, even in the most complicated of situations, our words can be heard and taken on with love.

Tanzanite works with all forms of communication, including dance, singing and the expressive arts. In all cases it can help us express our emotions clearly.

Physical: To support the physical body, place a small Tanzanite crystal on the throat once a week for 3–5 minutes. If it falls off before the time is up, that indicates the healing has ended.

Emotional: You may want to communicate how you feel, but you fear what the outcome will be. To support this process, find a Tanzanite specimen you are drawn to. Then for at least three days prior to the actual conversation start journaling on the following: *How do I feel about the conversation? What do I want to say? What do I want the outcome of the conversation to be?* Over time you will experience clarity around what you want to say.

Soul: One way to receive intuitive guidance is through *intuitive writing*. With its connection to the throat chakra, the heart and intuition, Tanzanite can help you cultivate these skills. Take a moment to relax the mind. Hold the crystal over your heart as you write your first question. Take a breath and then, on the exhale, start writing the answer, trusting that the words will come. At the start, you might need to ask your question more than once and even spell out the answers, but over time they will come more easily.

Additional properties: Self-expression, creative expression

Additional techniques: If you are cultivating new creative ideas, use Tanzanite to meditate and visualize the final idea.

Suggested shapes: Raw, jewellery

Source: Tanzania

TURQUOISE

ANCIENT WISDOM

Turquoise is a storm element crystal, holding all the elements (Earth, Fire, Air and Water) within it. Everything is made up of one or a mix of all of the elements, so Turquoise can support us in all areas of life.

It's also a wise grandfather crystal, an ancient stone that has been connected to humankind for thousands of years. Working with this timeless stone is like seeking guidance from the elder of a tribe; it offers insight that only someone who has lived a long life can give.

Physical: For physical support, start by placing your Turquoise crystal over the throat area. Then after a few minutes intuitively move the crystal around your body. Keep moving it until you naturally feel you have come to the end of the healing.

Emotional: Sometimes adult responsibilities can feel overwhelming and you want someone older and wiser to take over the decision-making for a while. If you select Turquoise for emotional support, that is what you are energetically requesting. When working with Turquoise, you will first notice its blue tones calming the nervous system, the stress dissipating as if someone else has taken over. Carry a Turquoise with you throughout the day. Try to keep it out on display so it's always visible. That way it can help relieve feelings of being overwhelmed so you can take control of the situation and make better decisions.

Soul: If you feel connected to Turquoise, it could be that it's time to explore the ancient cultures, beliefs and wisdoms of your native lands. All you have to do is keep Turquoise with you to attract information on your culture's traditions and practices. These insights can create a sense of belonging as well as unearthing innate skills that are available to you.

Additional properties: Promotes ancestral connection, welcomes insights, soul journeying

Additional techniques: Sleep with Turquoise nearby in order to connect to your spirit animal.

Suggested shapes: Carvings, jewellery, raw

Source: The USA, Iran, Mexico, Chile, China, the UK

AMETHYST

SPIRITUAL WOUNDS

Amethyst is probably the best-known third eye chakra crystal. It helps people decrease the intake of anything that is not good for them, resulting in a healthy and more relaxed constitution, leading to easier access to our intuition.

Physical: Amethyst is particularly helpful if you are suffering from ailments that do not have an obvious source. Place your crystal on the third eye. Ask your crystal what physical support your body needs. Exhale slowly and, if you get any physical sensation in the body, move your crystal to that area and ask it the same question again. Keep doing this until you receive clear guidance or feel the need to stop moving the crystal to new areas.

Emotional: Amethyst can also help us understand addictive behaviours, if there are blocks stopping us accessing our intuition or why we find it hard to relax. To understand more, use Amethyst in a crystal elixir (see page 26).

Soul: You may be ready to explore your intuitive and psychic abilities and release any past life trauma that is blocking them. This may be connected to witch wounds (see page 61). Carry out the following ritual to awaken your skills.

AMETHYST ANOINTING RITUAL

1. Before starting the ritual, consider having a relaxing bath, maybe adding an Amethyst to the bathwater to deepen your relaxed state.

2. After that, sit down and place a drop of lavender massage or facial oil on your crystal. Close your eyes and visualize your third eye chakra as a purple disc of light in between your eyebrows.

3. Place the side of your Amethyst that has the oil lightly against the third eye to activate it. Imagine a ray of light going from the crystal into your head, switching on your intuitive abilities.

4. Before you open your eyes, see the light go back into the crystal.

Additional properties: Accessing the violet ray, spiritual alchemy

Additional techniques: Add an Amethyst tumble to your bathwater to enjoy a healing bath.

Suggested shapes: Clusters, hearts, wands, natural points, bowls

Source: Worldwide

AMETRINE *also called Bolivianite*

SPIRITUAL BLOCKS

Citrine is created when Amethyst is heated naturally by the Earth's core or via human intervention. When we find both Amethyst and Citrine in the same crystal, that crystal is called Ametrine.

Together Amethyst and Citrine are a powerful combination, creating a strong manifestation energy. As we have seen (see page 102) one of Citrine's main properties is manifestation. Amethyst (see page 172) is famously the 'healing crystal', so it can clear away any blocks that might prevent your manifestations from materializing. The word 'block' refers to something that is holding us back from our goals. The chakra holding this block relates to the theme of your goal. Therefore, a third eye block might be connected to our intuition or spiritual growth. Ametrine is a third eye crystal that can be used to overcome any fears or blocks around trusting and listening to our intuition.

Physical: For five minutes a day, while lying down, place the crystal between your eyebrows, over the third eye. This is particularly good for releasing any tension in the face and can strengthen your mental health.

Emotional: If you feel you might be experiencing blocks that are stopping you from connecting to your intuition, try lying down with your eyes closed and taking some long, deep breaths. Then focus on the third eye and consider if the energy there feels light or heavy. If it's heavy, place the crystal on your third eye and visualize any extra energy in that area going into the crystal. After five minutes, remove the crystal. Lie there for a few more minutes before you get up.

Soul: You might be experiencing intuitive blocks that could have past-life, ancestral or other-life origins, so follow the emotional steps outlined above, but this time, when connecting to the block, also consider that it might show up in your auric field or as an object in your energetic field.

Additional properties: Success, goal setting, prosperity

Additional techniques: If you go to the gym, carry Ametrine in your pocket to help you improve performance.

Suggested shapes: Tumbles, points

Source: Bolivia

CHAROITE *also called Charoite Jade*

SPIRITUAL DISCERNMENT

Charoite's dramatic purple tones echo its powerful intuitive abilities, while the black indicates the root chakra energies of the physical world. Combine the two and this crystal helps us receive psychic messages through our physical body.

Depending on how we receive these messages, it can be hard to decipher if they are actually psychic or simply body fluctuations. This is often the case if you receive intuitive messages in the following ways:

Clairsentience: Feelings
Clairegustance: Taste
Clairalience: Smell

Charoite helps us refine these skills so we can differentiate.

Physical: The purple tones of Charoite focus on the head, while the black indicates the areas of the root chakra (from the hips down). Together they support our spatial awareness, including our sight and ailments such as vertigo. For support, try taking a Charoite elixir (see page 26) for at least 10 days.

Emotional: Do you think you might be receiving intuitive messages but dismiss them because you can't be sure they are genuine? Charoite will help you gain confidence in your psychic skills. To do this, wear Charoite jewellery regularly. Before bed, hold your jewellery and recite this affirmation at least three times: *I trust my intuition.*

Soul: When actively connecting to your intuition, either to receive guidance for yourself or to offer a reading for someone else, you can use Charoite to confirm you are receiving accurate messages. Hold a Charoite crystal in your dominant hand. When a message comes through, close your eyes and see how the body responds to it. Does the body feel *positive, uplifted, energetic, as if it is leaning forwards*? This is a sign a message is true. If you feel *sad, lacking energy or as if you want to shy away*, the message isn't correct.

Additional properties: Transformation, transmutes karma

Additional techniques: Wear Charoite to actively welcome more magic and synchronicities into your life.

Suggested shapes: Jewellery, tumbles

Source: Russia

LITHIUM QUARTZ

MIND CHATTER

Two things happen when we connect to Lithium Quartz: the energies of compassion and love open up to us, and our higher heart activates. At that point its healing energy comes up to the third eye, replacing any mind chatter, fears and anxieties with a feeling of profound peace. This activation of the third eye brings in the energies of our higher self and the wisdoms we have collected over lifetimes.

Physical: Lithium Quartz is the ideal crystal for supporting the physical health of the mind. Try placing it under your pillow at night, as the body mends itself while we sleep.

Emotional: Do you have a busy mind? If you observe it, do you witness it berating you or offering negative opinions about others? This can affect your mental health: the more negative thoughts you have, the lower your frequency will be. Working with Lithium Quartz will help you connect to the higher self, reducing and eventually eliminating those negative thoughts. To cultivate this change of perception, sleep with a Lithium Quartz under your pillow and another over your heart. If you enjoy the energy and want to keep a Lithium Quartz crystal with you during the day, you can wear it in the form of earrings or a necklace.

Soul: Selecting Lithium Quartz for your spiritual goals suggests that your higher self wants to offer you intuitive guidance. To cultivate this skill, meditate with a Lithium Quartz crystal in your dominant hand. Then imagine a line of lithium energy surrounding your auric field. Breathe in that energy and breathe out any mind chatter. Once you feel relaxed, in your mind's eye ask a question, then press your crystal to your third eye and allow the answer to come as a train of thought.

Additional properties: Helps with grief and abandonment, supports the end-of-life transition

Additional techniques: To bring a relationship into balance, have both parties carry a Lithium Quartz tumble.

Suggested shapes: Mini points, clusters, tumbles, jewellery

Source: Brazil

PURPLE FLUORITE

CLARITY

All fluorite crystals improve our focus. They are perfect for those who find study hard, who find themselves easily distracted or whose jobs require a high level of accuracy – for example doctors, scientists, statisticians and those in the financial industry.

Purple Fluorite is particularly good for these activities because its colour frequency matches that of the third eye and the mind.

Physical: To use Purple Fluorite as a physical support place three crystals in a triangle on your third eye. Leave them there for 15 minutes several times a week.

Emotional: Purple Fluorite can best support mind clarity when you keep a specimen beside you as you work. You might also want to source a smaller Purple Fluorite crystal that you can carry at work or keep with you when you are out and about.

Soul: Selecting Purple Fluorite as your spiritual crystal suggests you are receiving intuitive guidance and divine inspiration. However, you may be receiving so many messages that it's hard to identify the best ones. If this feels like you, drinking a Purple Fluorite elixir daily will help offer more clarity (see page 26).

Additional properties: Supports study, retaining or expanding your knowledge

Additional techniques: To help recall information when taking an exam, carry a small Purple Fluorite specimen in your pocket.

Suggested shapes: Points, palms, sacred geometry sets, chips

Source: Worldwide

SPIRIT QUARTZ

also called Fairy Quartz, Cactus Quartz

CHANNELLING

A channel is a person who can receive large amounts of intuitive information, normally through clairaudience (hearing) or clairvoyance (seeing), but also as sudden downloads of information. As you raise your vibration these moments of pure inspiration will start to become available to you.

Spirit Quartz is a member of the amethyst family. All amethysts open our third eye to help us access our intuition, but Spirit Quartz then progresses this ability, forming a channel so that deeper wisdom and insights can enter.

Physical: Most crystals that support our third eye also look after our physical eyesight. Closing your eyes and placing a small Spirit Quartz point over each one will offer them a chance to heal and release any tension that might be building up.

Emotional: If you feel you are intuitive but can't truly commit to following the guidance you receive, this could be because you feel you are not worthy, or due to latent fears relating to how people will receive the message. In those cases, try displaying a large Spirit Quartz specimen where you channel. It can then act as an intuition coach, creating a space to receive messages and helping you to interpret them correctly. If you do readings for others, you can also display an Amazonite specimen next to it (see page 122), to activate your higher heart so you can relay the messages with diplomacy.

Soul: The energy of Spirit Quartz transcends our normal third eye abilities, opening us up to higher energies so we can receive more profound messages. We need to activate our causal chakra, which is positioned behind the head about 5cm (2in) above us, to help filter higher energy frequencies as they enter the body. To support this, sleep with a Spirit Quartz crystal underneath your pillow.

Additional properties: Offers spiritual protection, connects you to the plant spirits

Additional techniques: Sleep with a Spirit Quartz by your bedside if you want to connect to the fairy kingdom.

Suggested shapes: Raw

Source: South Africa

SUGILITE

SPIRITUAL PROTECTION

Sugilite is a protective crystal for the unseen world. It allows us to work confidently with our psychic skills to receive guidance, dispelling any negative energies and only letting the purest energies through. It also clears energy from a room and a person's auric field, so it's easier to connect to their energies and offer them a psychic reading.

Physical: When we don't know the source of the problem or perhaps there is a 'phantom pain' lingering for no obvious reason, this crystal is perfect. Place Sugilite over the third eye and imagine a ray of violet light leaving the crystal and going to the painful area. Allow the whole area to be surrounded by the crystal's energy and then see the violet ray going back to the crystal, taking the pain with it.

Emotional: Do you feel drained after spending time with specific people or in specific locations? Do you have unexplained negative emotions or seem to mirror someone's emotions after spending time with them? If so, wearing Sugilite will help you retain your energies and stop this from happening. Try also using Sugilite with Black Obsidian (page 62) and Selenite (page 202) as part of your energetic hygiene practice, particularly if you find these situations are really affecting you.

Soul: Selecting Sugilite suggests that spiritual alchemy might be a skill available to you, meaning you might have innate but dormant abilities to access the elements and different healing energies. Sugilite also has an affinity to the violet flame, so it can transmute negativity and turn it into a positive frequency. Simply hold your crystal over your heart and imagine it turning into a violet flame burning eternally in your heart. Once lit, this light will stay with you, but you can still make the gesture of touching the Sugilite to your heart when you actively want to transmute negative energy.

Additional properties: Removes negative attachments, promotes lucid dreaming

Additional techniques: Wear as earrings when you are ready to remember your soul purpose.

Suggested shapes: Raw, jewellery

Sources: Canada, South Africa

APOPHYLLITE *also called Fisheye Stone*

RITUAL

When it comes to working on our goals, where we choose to work can really affect our mood and efficiency. Apophyllite creates an atmosphere that is perfect for healing. Its white and transparent look indicates its connection to the crown chakra and therefore to our spirituality. It also often has transparent areas that then transition to opaque features, indicating it can help bring our spirituality into the physical world.

Physical: When you know you have been overdoing it or your body needs time to focus on healing, place an Apophyllite specimen above your head and a second one below your feet. This very quickly allows the body's frequency to relax and enter a state of *rest and digest*.

Emotional: Perhaps you need to cultivate the perfect space that will support your progression. For example, if you are in a busy house, the tranquil energies of Apophyllite will create an energetic barrier, offering you privacy and time away from other people's energies. Consider where you like to journal, meditate, contemplate or carry out healing work. Then find an Apophyllite specimen you can display there to hold the energies for you.

Soul: A lot of people cultivating a spiritual practice also create an altar space. This is a table or platform displaying items such as statues, photos, crystals and sage, and sometimes objects that represent our aspirations or dreams. This space becomes the centre of our spiritual practice.

Creating a place like this might help keep you focused on your goals. Start by pinpointing a space in your home for your altar that you can visit regularly and display your Apophyllite there. Then take a few weeks to add other items, testing them in the space before committing to displaying them there, carrying out activities like journaling, meditation, yoga and prayer.

Additional properties: Astral projection, connection to your spirit guides, guidance on your past, present or future

Additional techniques: Place an Apophyllite pyramid on your third eye to take back any energy you have unknowingly given to others.

Suggested shapes: Clusters, natural pyramids

Source: Worldwide

CLEAR QUARTZ *also called Rock Crystal*

RECEIVING KNOWLEDGE

Clear Quartz is one of the most popular and versatile crystals, because it can be programmed to support you in any way you want. As a clear, transparent crystal, it can allow light to pass through it. This light is made up of every colour of the rainbow, meaning it can support all of the chakras and any issues you may have.

To program Clear Quartz, sit and hold your crystal in your non-dominant hand. Close your eyes and relax your breath. Then consider how you want Clear Quartz to support you. After that, imagine your crystal has helped you achieve that goal. Think about what life would be like when that has happened and how you would feel. Then open your eyes. When your crystal has done its job, simply cleanse it (see pages 10–11) and then you can program it with another task.

Physical: To support the area of the crown chakra, traditionally Clear Quartz is placed on a pillow above the head. If your crystal has a point, have it facing away from your head to alleviate pain, fogginess or fatigue.

Emotional: Sometimes our goals are very specific to our needs, so there isn't always an ideal crystal for them. In this case, a programmed crystal would be the best option to support you. Simply follow the steps above to program your crystals, then keep it with you as an emotional support.

Soul: Ancient civilizations are believed to have programmed Clear Quartz crystals with their knowledge. Selecting this crystal suggests that the information you need might be hidden in it. Try taking a moment to see if it might have some information to offer you, by first sitting with the crystal in your dominant hand. Relax completely, then, in your mind's eye, ask the crystal if it has any information for you and see if an answer comes.

Additional properties: Cleanses and amplifies other crystals

Additional techniques: When things are going well, carry a Clear Quartz crystal to increase your success.

Suggested shapes: Natural and polished points, skulls, sacred geometry sets, wands, clusters

Source: Worldwide

ELESTIAL QUARTZ

also called Skeletal Quartz, Jacare Quartz

ASCENSION

You might have heard the terms 'entering the Age of Aquarius' or 'moving from 3D to 5D'. Both terms refer to the next stage of human evolution as predicted by many channels, as well as by ancient civilizations such as the Mayans. This evolution isn't so much a physical change as a rise in our vibration so that we can live from a happier, more compassionate place. Elestial Quartz helps with this ascension process. Its multiple points send out its energy into different directions so we can find the right way forwards.

Physical and Emotional: Elestial Quartz offers a deep clearing and healing, including the releasing of old karma, so you can work towards living from this higher state of consciousness. To work with Elestial Quartz to support your physical or emotional body, follow the soul steps below, but this time have the points of the crystal facing away from the body.

Soul: Selecting Elestial Quartz as your soul plan crystal suggests you are ready to raise your vibration. Many small changes collectively make that shift in energy happen, and supporting the energy body and working with crystals will have you heading in the right direction.

Elestial Quartz helps us access other dimensions. This can include creating a connection with the angels or our spirit guides, spending time with our ancestors or even connecting to other galaxies. It could also include spending more time living in the fifth dimension. To create this connection before you sleep at night, place your Elestial Quartz safely above your head, pointing towards your crown. Stay there for a maximum of 20 minutes. Only follow this process when it's safe for you to feel drowsy the next day, as you may experience busy dreams or a sleepless night.

Additional properties: Connects you to the angelic realm and other galaxies

Additional techniques: Those who want to pursue a career in science fiction or abstract expression might want to display this crystal in their creative space to welcome forwards original concepts.

Suggested shapes: Raw

Source: Brazil

GODDESS STONE

also called Fairy Stone, Menalite

DIVINE GUIDANCE

This crystal helps us deepen our meditation skills, allowing us to practise sustained periods of contemplation and prayer that will help us to cultivate a relationship with a specific god or goddess. The Goddess Stone also helps us access the energies of the Divine Feminine. This is closely entwined with the spirit world and our intuition, so cultivating that part of us welcomes in more divine insights and judgement.

Physical: This crystal is a calcium-rich mineral, so taking it as an elixir (see page 26) can strengthen our bodies. Its association with the Goddess suggests that a Goddess Stone elixir will stabilize our hormones, as well as supporting fertility and all stages of pregnancy.

Emotional: The Goddess Stone honours the cycles of life, as well as other cycles we experience. We can be drawn to a Goddess Stone when we have reached the end of a particularly difficult, traumatic stage of our life and it's time to start afresh. For divine guidance for the path ahead, try using oracle cards. Source a deck you are drawn to and shuffle the cards so they are connected to your energy. Then leave the cards overnight with your Goddess Stone placed on top. The following morning, think of a question as you shuffle the cards again, then choose one or more cards to receive the answer. If you have more questions, think of them as you draw more cards. Once you're done, place your crystal on top of the cards again to sustain the energies.

Soul: The Goddess Stone can also come into our life when it's time to connect more deeply and work with a deity we are drawn to. Often deities communicate with us through symbols we see in the everyday world. To understand the symbol your god or goddess will use to communicate to you, place your Goddess Stone by your bed before sleep. Have the intention that you will wake up in the morning knowing what your symbol will be.

Additional properties: The Divine Feminine, supports puberty, childbirth and the menopause

Additional techniques: Display Goddess Stone as a talisman when you want to understand and then fully embody anything classed as a feminine trait.

Suggested shapes: Raw

Source: Canada, Greenland, the UK, Morocco

HERKIMER DIAMOND

also called Little Falls Diamond, Middleville Diamond

CONNECTION

If you are not religious, it can be hard to understand why cultivating a connection to Source Energy (also called the Universe, the Divine or God) is so important. When we reincarnate, we forget about our past lives and where we go in between so that we can fully learn the lessons our current life offers. However, this act of forgetting can create an unexplainable sadness or loneliness.

Selecting this crystal suggests you need to open the crown chakra further. When we fully open this chakra, some of us start to remember, whereas others feel the loneliness being replaced by a profound connection to something greater. Herkimer Diamonds can help strengthen that connection, as they have an innate ability to funnel energies through them, either away or into the body.

Physical: To welcome healing energies into the body, place a Herkimer Diamond above the crown of the head. Position it so that one tip is facing your crown and the other is facing away. Leave it there for three minutes. Do this once a week for a month.

Emotional: Herkimer Diamonds offer great support when you are regaining and strengthening your connection to Source Energy. Follow the steps above for physical support and, while the crystal is in place, focus on the breath. On the exhale, imagine old emotions leaving your body through the crown and going up into the sky. On the inhale, imagine new, more positive emotions entering your body.

Soul: When we are reconnected to Source Energy we can receive intuitive messages and guidance from higher planes. To welcome this guidance, follow the physical steps above. On the inhale, imagine white light coming down from the Universe, into the crown and then the third eye. On the exhale, imagine that light going from the third eye, through the crown, back up to the Universe.

Additional properties: Discernment, clearing energy fields, soul retrieval

Additional techniques: Place a Herkimer Diamond by your newest crystal purchase to cultivate a connection with it and understand how you should work with it.

Suggested shapes: Raw

Source: New York

HOWLITE

MEDITATION

Howlite could be mistaken for a piece of white marble. Its energies offer a similar, regal air that embodies grand stately homes and government buildings. However, placing Howlite in a space creates a very different atmosphere. This is the crystal of meditation. Displaying it in your home cultivates a quiet, serene space, perfect for relaxation and contemplation.

Physical: Selecting Howlite for physical support indicates that the body would benefit from some respite. Find some time in your diary when you can step back and relax. On those days of rest, either wear Howlite or drink it as an indirect crystal elixir (see page 26). This helps the body move quickly into the parasympathetic mode of *rest and digest*.

Emotional: Meditating can be hard. Mind chatter can take over and make sitting in silence difficult. Ensuring that we are as calm as possible will help to overcome this. When we are awake we are operating from a beta brainwave state, which moves up to high beta when we are stressed. To meditate we need to be in a theta state, which is the same as light sleep.

Howlite's energy resembles the theta frequency. Therefore, holding it in your dominant hand when you start meditating will aid in calming the mind and body so you can deepen your practice.

Soul: Once you have cultivated a meditation routine, you can start enhancing this practice. Some people use meditation as a time for contemplation. In these circumstances, once you are relaxed, you can shift your attention from keeping your mind clear of thought to welcoming in any intuitive guidance that might be available to you.

To start the flow of information, try meditating lying down. Place a Howlite crystal on the pillow above your head so it can expand the energies of the crown chakra, making it easier for you to receive messages.

Additional properties: Insomnia, stress relief, combating loneliness

Additional techniques: When you feel overwhelmed with work, carry a Howlite worry stone with you to help focus the mind on the most urgent task.

Suggested shapes: Palm stones, worry stones

Source: Canada, the USA, Turkey, Mexico

LIMESTONE

RECONNECTION

Sometimes some of the most powerful crystal energies are right beneath our feet, so when we connect to Mother Earth, it is often their energies we are feeling. These can be the stones and crystals that make up our buildings, that form famous monuments and comprise vast amounts of the Earth's surface. Limestone was used to build some of the most famous structures in the world, such as the Great Pyramids of Giza. The history of this often under-appreciated stone is closely entwined with our own.

Physical: Selecting Limestone may be a reminder to stay connected to your body, to honour and love it. It suggests you might not always appreciate it, or be happy with how it performs or how it looks, but it's time to see past that and honour it as the gift that it is. Ask yourself each day, *What can I do right now as an act of self-love for my body?* Whatever the answer is, make time in your day to do it.

Emotional: Many on the spiritual path can feel lost, depressed or as if they don't belong. Limestone asks that you consider the following: *If you had a monument dedicated to you, what would you want it to say?* Today is the day to sit down and make plans so you can achieve the kind of goals you would want engraved into that stone.

Soul: Perhaps it's time for you to reconnect to ancient lands and civilizations from previous lives. Consider booking a session to open your Akashic Records (which store all the information of our soul experiences) or try past-life regression so you can remember previous teachings and start using them in this life. Start on this journey by sourcing your own Limestone specimen to display as a talisman to welcome in this exploratory work.

Additional properties: Strength, reliability, loyalty

Additional techniques: Meditate in close proximity to a famous limestone structure to see if you can receive information about its creation and uses.

Suggested shapes: Raw

Source: Worldwide

SCOLECITE

PEACE

If you can imagine a crystal emanating deep inner peace, it will start to explain the subtle but impactful energies of Scolecite. In its natural form, Scolecite is made up of multiple rods, but it can also be faceted into different shapes. Raw specimens are fragile, so a Scolecite palm stone will be easier to work with.

Physical: Scolecite connects the body to the energies of peace. This connection washes away everyday stresses, so we can enhance our *chi*, the life force energy running through our bodies. Source a specimen you are particularly drawn to and display it in a place of prominence so your body can enjoy its energy throughout the day.

Emotional: Spending time on our own helps us understand ourselves, become familiar with our own energies and learn to enjoy our own company. Selecting Scolecite invites you to consider some alone time. If this makes you feel anxious, try starting with an afternoon or evening, before committing to a full day or weekend. If you feel you might not like the silences, carry your crystal with you for a few days beforehand so it can slowly introduce you to these new energies and prepare you for being on your own for longer.

Soul: There are many definitions of *enlightenment*, but in essence they all speak about a moment when the soul fully reconnects to Source Energy, offering a profound level of joy and deep inner peace. If you want to work towards this goal, try displaying these three crystals in your home: Scolecite, which offers the energy of divine peace; Citrine, which has the property of pure joy; and a type of Clear Quartz known as Samadhi Quartz, *samadhi* being Sanskrit for 'enlightened'. Each day look at these three crystals and decide which one (or ones) you want to keep with you that day.

Additional properties: Balance, universal consciousness, healing the planet

Additional techniques: Display a Scolecite sphere in the living room to promote a harmonious household.

Suggested shapes: Raw, spheres, jewellery, tumbles

Source: India, Iceland, Australia

SELENITE *also called Gypsum*

ENERGETIC CLEARING

The name Selenite is derived from Selene, the Greek goddess of the Moon. Therefore, it is no surprise that this crystal is used to connect us to the Moon, the cycles of life and the energies connected to the Divine Feminine.

Physical: Selenite can be used to reduce headaches, foggy head or pressure in the head. Place three rods above the head, one end pointing towards the crown, the others pointing away. Leave them there for 20 minutes so the rods can calm the mind and direct the energy away from the crown.

Emotional: An empath is someone who takes on the emotions of other people. People don't always realize that they are an empath, however, so they don't understand that the emotions they are feeling are not their own. Instead, it can feel as if they're going from one emotional extreme to another. If this resonates with you, consider who you are with when these emotions arise. Then try to identify ways to release these emotions. One option is the energetic hygiene practice given below.

Soul: Spiritual hygiene describes the practice of clearing unwanted energy and emotions from our auric field. For this practice, first source a Selenite wand that is at least 10cm (4in) long, then hold it at one end. To *brush the aura*, hold the wand about 5cm (2in) away from your body and move it along in a brushing motion. At the same time, have the intention that you are clearing anything in the auric space.

Make sure your brushstrokes go from the centre of your body up over your head, or from the centre down to your feet. Flick the wand at the end of a brushstroke to clear the energy.

For a full energy clearing, include the Black Obsidian cord-cutting practice on page 62.

Additional properties: Cleansing, Divine Feminine, balancing emotions

Additional techniques: Keep a Selenite tumble in your pocket on a New or Full Moon as a way of accessing the Moon's energies.

Suggested shapes: Spheres, bowls, carvings

Source: The USA, Mexico

TOURMALATED QUARTZ
also called Tourmaline in Quartz

SPIRITUAL INTEGRATION

This wise crystal, made up of Black Tourmaline inside Clear Quartz, encapsulates one of spirituality's most provocative and thought-provoking concepts, *that Heaven on Earth is possible*! The etheric nature of Clear Quartz represents spirituality, the crown chakra and, in this context, Heaven. In contrast, the Black Tourmaline rods found inside the Clear Quartz represent the physical world, the root chakra and the Earth.

With each of these qualities wrapped around the other, this crystal holds the energies we need to make this dream a reality for everyone.

Physical: To strengthen and combine the physical and energetic body, source a Tourmalated Quartz crystal, a Clear Quartz crystal and a Black Tourmaline. Simply lie down with the Black Tourmaline beneath your feet, then place a Clear Quartz crystal above your head. When you are settled, place the Tourmalated Quartz over your heart. This draws the energies from the other two crystals to the centre of your body to combine and balance them.

Emotional: Do you believe you deserve to be happy and fulfilled, to have your own Heaven on Earth? Selecting this crystal suggests this is a concept that, once taken on, could offer big changes in your life. To do this, create a crystal grid (see page 25) that has a Tourmalated Quartz sphere specimen as your centre stone. Use the shape of an infinity spiral to create this grid. Half of the spiral needs to be all Black Tourmaline to represent the physical world, the other half should be Clear Quartz to represent the spiritual realm. Your Tourmalated Quartz then sits in the middle.

Soul: Selecting Tourmalated Quartz can also signal a desire to live more from our higher self or soul. Wearing Tourmalated Quartz jewellery starts to advance the connection between the physical and the energetic bodies in order to make this possible.

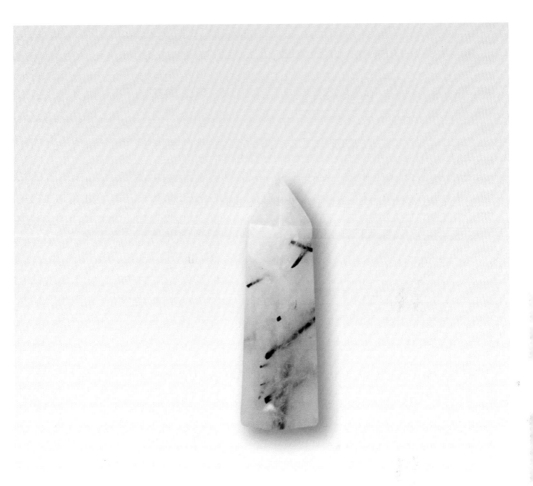

Additional properties: Grounding, transmuting energies, balancing opposing energies

Additional techniques: To release energy blocks, intuitively move a tumble around the body while meditating.

Suggested shapes: Spheres, towers, palms

Source: Brazil

WHITE OPAL

ENERGY BODY INTEGRATION

Since Roman times, White Opal has symbolized hope and love. With its connection to the crown chakra, the energy of love it offers is often described as a heavenly one. The rainbow light displayed in a White Opal suggests a connection to all the chakras. This crystal will keep increasing in popularity as humans continue to raise their vibration and shift into a more positive, community- and environment-focused global population. Wearing White Opal is a symbol of supporting this change.

Physical: Raising our vibrations can affect our physical body as we adjust to heightened energies. This can result in symptoms such as vertigo, dizziness or nausea. If you are experiencing these, always visit the doctor first, but you can also wear White Opal if you intuitively feel it might be connected to these changes.

Emotional: Have you ever questioned whether you are a spiritual being, having a physical experience? If you are having those thoughts or want to understand experiencing things from a higher perspective, source a White Opal. Place it on each chakra, one at a time for two minutes. Start at the crown, the most etheric energy; then move down through the chakras to the root chakra, which represents the physical world. Then move up the chakras again, but this time stop at the heart. Ask your heart for guidance and see what messages come through.

Soul: White Opal can be used to restore our energy body. As a powerful Water element crystal, the best method to do this is through elixirs. To create something special, set yourself a bath, with candles, incense and relaxing music. While the bath fills up, keep your crystal close by. This will turn the water into a White Opal elixir bath (see page 26) which will cleanse and restore all aspects of your energy body.

Additional properties: Emotional support, healing spiritual blocks, releasing stored emotions

Additional techniques: Place your White Opal over each chakra to strengthen the connection between the physical and the energetic body.

Suggested shapes: Raw, jewellery

Source: Australia, Brazil, Ethiopia

About the Author

Gemma Petherbridge set out on her spiritual path as a small child, prophesizing in her dreams. Seeing spirits, naturally intuiting situations and gaining insight into the destinies of others came as second nature, and after losing her parents at a young age she turned to spirituality for answers. Her journey into the world of wellness and holistic therapies began in earnest when, aged 23, she studied hypnotherapy.

Seventeen years on, Gemma is a Certified Crystal Healer, Intuition Teacher and Akashic Records Reader. Having transitioned from healer to teacher, she has now taught and inspired thousands of people worldwide. In 2017 she founded Conscience Crystals, which offers workshops, courses and an online shop. With her growing following, Gemma is now regularly asked to lead workshops and speak at holistic events and festivals, and major international businesses seek her guidance in incorporating crystals into office environments and products. She also presents the spiritual and holistic wellbeing podcast Higher Self School Podcast. Her first crystal book, *The Crystal Apothecary* launched worldwide in 2022, with her Crystal Mystery School launching in 2024.

Instagram: @gemmapetherbridge
Website: gemmapetherbridge.com

Acknowledgements

To Nicky, Leanne, Louisa, Yasia, Lisa, Giulia, Jen and the whole Octopus Publishing Group team. Thank you for this opportunity and for your continued support. You are always a joy to work with.

I would also like to thank the photographers Holly Booth of Holly Booth Studio and Sarah Ann Wright of Sarah Ann Wright Photography, as well as copyeditor Caroline Taggart.

The final thank yous must go to my husband and best friend, Russ, my sister, Sam, and my dear friend, Rachel for your ongoing support.

Love Gem